# COURAGE TO CARE

*— Lessons from Assisi —*

## GILLIAN T.W. AHLGREN

Contemplative
Wisdom for
Today

May you go forward
securely, joyfully, and swiftly,
on the path of prudent happiness,
believing nothing,
agreeing with nothing
that would dissuade you from this commitment
or would place a stumbling block for you on the way,
so that nothing prevents you from offering yourself
to the Most High in the perfection
to which the Spirit of God has called you.

**Clare of Assisi**

# CONTENTS

# Introduction

This book makes a case, a plea and a prayer for metanoia—a total change of mind, heart, perspective, will and action—in our day. Most people I know are deeply troubled by the direction that our world is going. What is worse, despite our unease, the chaos of our current reality seems to have the better hand. People of conscience, people in education, social service, and other fields with deep commitments to the common good, lean forward and confide, "I can't watch the news any more." "I'm troubled and anxious and don't even know why." "I don't know what to do to make a difference." We are disheartened, and any momentum toward another way seems to get very little traction.

For years now climate scientists have described and warned us of "tipping points," irreversible changes in the climate system. Since the 1960s, the term has been used in economics, human ecology, sociology, and epidemiology—but not usually in theology or spirituality. I remember perfectly the moment when I first sensed a pope using the concept. It was in late 2013, as we watched to see whether or not Jorge Bergoglio, history's first pope to ever take the name Francis, would live up to the legacy of his namesake. We knew something was afoot in his first interview, when his response to "Who are you? Who is Jorge Bergoglio?" was, "I am a sinner." At his request, religious communities with housing in the Vatican organized showers, laundry, and respite for the homeless. His first departure from the Vatican was to Lampedusa, where he mourned the passing of refugees whose small boat, overwhelmed with weight, had sunk. He shook his head in bewildered grief: "The Mediterranean is becoming a graveyard." And then his first major work, the Apostolic Exhortation The Joy of the Gospel. I sat up straight when I read:

> It is not the task of the Pope to offer a detailed and complete analysis of contemporary reality, but I do exhort all the communities to an "ever watchful scrutiny of the signs of the times". This is in fact a grave responsibility, since certain present realities, unless effectively dealt with, are capable of setting off processes of dehumanization which would then be hard to reverse. We need to distinguish clearly what might be a fruit of the kingdom from what runs counter to God's plan. This involves not only recognizing and discerning spirits, but also – and this is decisive – choosing movements of the spirit of good and rejecting those of the spirit of evil. (Pope Francis, *Joy of the Gospel*, paragraph 51)

The clarity in his prophetic words mingled with his hopeful affirmation:

> No one can strip us of the dignity bestowed upon us by God's boundless and unfailing love. With a tenderness which never disappoints, but is always capable of restoring our joy, Christ makes it possible for us to lift up our heads and to start anew. Let us not flee from the resurrection of Jesus, let us never give up, come what will. May nothing inspire more than his life, which impels us onwards! (Pope Francis, *Joy of the Gospel*, par. 3)

And then the clarion call: we are summoned to a "revolution of tenderness" by the God who became one of us.

For years, "tenderness" was the word I had associated with the revolutionary lives of Francis of Assisi (1182-1226) and Clare of Assisi (1193-1253), two of Christianity's most beloved saints. In 2014 I dusted off an unfinished manuscript that I had set aside, thinking that the last thing the world needed was another book about Francis and Clare. Now I felt a deepening sense of urgency: Are we truly approaching more tipping points than we acknowledge? Environmental tipping points, of course, but also social and political ones, as we lose the habits of diplomacy, of civility, of communal deliberation, and so many other forms of human interaction that are necessary for collaboration. And human tipping points, as empathy gives rise to fear, humility to impunity, inquiry to conviction, listening to grandstanding, learning to parroting, intimacy and love to tinder. Are we going to simply stand by, watching our own dehumanization and allowing ourselves to rob and be robbed of creativity, wisdom, compassion and joy?

Perhaps what we need most of all is a way of proceeding. A way that cuts through the madness of our current ways with a tried-and-true method for the deepest kinds of changes that human beings can make. We need to know, with certainty, that there is another way, and we need to see that other way in action. Insofar as we can understand the steps in a process of change toward that other way, so much the better. Pope Francis's Joy of the Gospel gave me confidence to begin to voice questions about our world that Francis and Clare asked and answered in theirs: Is it possible that the very challenges that we face have the capacity to call us to a different way of experiencing our humanity? Will we succumb to the habits of greed and violence that keep us from exploring and developing the tenderness that makes us humane? Is it time to try a different way?

The life of Francis of Assisi shows us brilliantly a revolutionary way of tenderness, open to us if we are willing to risk "falling in love in a quite absolute, final way." Yet even for Francis, the way toward a life of authenticity and joy was not obvious. As a young man deeply disturbed by what he had seen and experienced in war, Francis wandered through a nagging dissatisfaction and emptiness until, as he himself tells us, "God led me into a leper colony." There, in a space where he least expected it, Francis fell in love with the living God. And a whole new way of life began.

In a world as needy as ours is today, how and where might such a revolution begin? We have lost contact with nature. We have lost genuine connection with others; even our relationships with friends and loved ones are often stretched thin by daily stresses and are in need of deep renewal. We are beleaguered by the pace and challenges of daily living. And, after a global pandemic and with political polarization threatening to torpedo any genuine dialogue toward the common good, many of us no longer hold out hope that human goodness will carry the day.

While no one is capable of solving the problems we ourselves have generated, we are fortunate to have the example of two individuals who, together and with radical complementarity, inspired a true "revolution" in their day. Francis and Clare of Assisi, two of Christianity's most well-known saints, were widely considered universal examples of human goodness during their day. Their decision to live the gospel way in radical simplicity and purity of heart has not only inspired millions over the centuries but provides a viable way for us to recover the fullness of our humanity today.

Francis and Clare's way of life helps us to discover the One who walks with us; the One who shares our burdens, our suffering, and our joy; and the One who gives us the hope, strength, and courage to work together toward a world that is home for all. This loving way of life that seeks encounter, collaboration,



*Gillian T.W. Ahlgren*

solidarity and communion can "liberate us from our narrowness and self-absorption" and provide us with fresh ways of seeing both the challenges and the possibilities of human life in the 21st century. As Pope Francis reminded us over ten years ago:

> We become fully human when we become more than human, when we let God bring us beyond ourselves in order to attain the fullest truth of our being... For if we have received the love which restores meaning to our lives, how can we fail to share that love with others? (Pope Francis, *Joy of the Gospel*, par. 8)

Ironically, it is our honesty about our own human needs and longings that can awaken and motivate us in the movement toward radical change. We all need to love and be loved; we all long to love and be loved. There is nothing more practical or basic to humanity than that. When that need and that longing come together, with sincerity, simplicity, and intensity, a new way of life comes alive. And that new way of life is more critical now than ever, for the world around us cries out its need for love and its need for the total change of mind and heart that genuine love propels.

Despite the chaos and strife in our world, there remains a piece of radically good news: we have the capacity to know and to share life-giving love. We can learn love, from God and from one another, as we share life together in graced encounter. Francis of Assisi's realization of God's nearness, known through the tenderness of loving human encounter, was the key to the revolutionary way of life still available to us today. Francis and Clare model for us "the revolution of tenderness," the gospel way that tells us to "risk face-to-face encounter with others, with their physical presence which challenges us, with their pain and their pleas, with their joy which infects us in our close and continuous interaction." (Pope Francis, *Joy of the Gospel*, par. 88)   Learning to recognize and collaborate with the presence of God in the world around us gives us access to a joy no one can take from us.

We ought not allow ourselves to be robbed of the joy of life, the joy of being human and of sharing life together—the joy that love, in all its shapes and forms, bestows. Today we are even more confused than ever about what true joy is. And I suspect that such confusion stems from an even deeper uncertainty about love—what it is, where to find it, how to cultivate it, what to do when one no longer feels it. When we have lost the basic practices of community—meal sharing, fellowship, conversations about what matters most to us, and simply being present to one another—how can we expect to find what it is that we most want? Our very humanity is being rewritten for us by the relentless demands of technology, a consumptive culture, and the contempt, for people and for goodness, that we see being modeled in government and global affairs. We need to recover the graces of a deeply relational culture in which we make time for meaningful companionship and create together the world we dream of.

In this book I invite you to walk with me in the footsteps of Francis and Clare and consider how their vision might contain seeds of change that we, in today's world, can appropriate. I want to open up their journey of radical change for our contemplation so that we can, like they did, recognize God in our midst—the One Who walks and works with us as we create the life that we long for. Francis's and Clare's path is one of radical simplicity that opens the heart and helps us to see what truly matters. Walking with them may give us new ways to engage our own challenges, learn love afresh, and nurture the presence of God in one another and in our world. Our times need hearts that are true and strong, courageous and faithful.

                                    *Gillian T.W. Ahlgren*

For when such hearts join together, infused by the energy of the Spirit, we are empowered in the love that provides hope, strength, and new possibility.

The message of Francis and Clare, like that of the One whom they followed, is both demanding and liberating. To let Francis and Clare speak to us directly is to listen to a message that, like the gospel, will change who we are. Their words point to a more authentic way of living out our relationship with God and with one another. If we find Francis and Clare's spirituality authentic, then we must listen to what they have to teach us about God. For their God is a God who might surprise us; the Christian community they invite us to join is one that might look somewhat different from the one in which we currently participate. Francis and Clare asked their contemporaries to do hard things: to reach out in love to the leper and the marginalized; to recognize, in poverty and simplicity, the face of Christ in the other; to move past superficialities in order to find and revere, protect and defend the God who is pulsing in the heart of a suffering world.

This book is a new iteration of my earlier monograph, *The Tenderness of God: Reclaiming Our Humanity* (Fortress Press, 2017). Much of the material in that monograph has been reorganized along the lines of metanoia—the change of heart, mind and life that our world cries out for. Having guided hundreds of people in the footsteps of Francis and Clare in Assisi over the years, I continue to see and be inspired by the many ways that Assisi changes people. Francis and Clare speak clearly, directly across the centuries, to our world today. I am deeply grateful to Will Bergkamp at Fortress Press for his creative solution that both honors the integrity of *The Tenderness of God* and allows me the opportunity to send a new iteration of these words into the world.

Whoever you are, I hope that this book offers a theological and spiritual synthesis of contemporary relevance. I would like to thank those who have walked with me over the years on my Spiritual Immersion Experiences; our conversations have been critical to the slow process of finding words for what matters most to us. Some of my reflections from those immersion experiences are integrated into this book. You'll recognize them as the italicized passages.

Whether this book serves as your initial introduction to the lives of Francis and Clare or whether you have already been drawn closer to God because of them, I hope that this book serves as food for your ongoing journey.



*Gillian T.W. Ahlgren*

# 1

# Seeking Something More:
# Searching and Journeying Together

What happens when we take seriously our sense that there has to be something more to our lives than what we are currently experiencing? Whenever we instinctually know that our lives, individually and collectively, are not entirely working, our dissatisfaction, whether with our personal circumstances or with the world in which we live, can become the seed of change and creative possibility. When we recognize, with sincerity and integrity, our desire for greater meaning, coherence, and purpose in our lives, we are already creating space for something new. Then, for the sake of our own well-being, we engage a genuine process of searching, a journey that leads us to probe what it means to be human and how to be related to others. For as we begin to speak more honestly about our longings for fullness of life, we often come to find out that we are not alone in them. A movement toward goodness, sharing, improvement and collaboration, that grows as we do, fueled by sincerity, honesty, humility and a genuine desire to understand things from a different vantage point, can be born.

The hungers of our hearts intuitively know what truly feeds us and what does not. But it can take significant discipline to orient our daily lives around what is truly life-giving. Honestly distinguishing between what we most deeply want and what we so readily settle for is a great help in discarding what keeps us from being free to create the life that we long for. Sometimes the very circumstances of our lives compel us to ask ourselves what truly matters to us and what does not. The very chaos of our current reality awakens us to our need for meaning and coherence, which turns out to be nearly as critical as our daily bread.

For both Francis and Clare, dissatisfaction with life reached in deep. Their journey toward a life of purpose, meaning and joy epitomizes St. Augustine's succinct observation about the human condition: "Our hearts are restless until they find their rest in You." And they model for us how to live out the spiritual journey with integrity as people who seek to move forward, step by step, toward a more humane world, a more authentic human community. As a person who has led immersive experiences in the footsteps of Francis and Clare in Assisi for many years, I have been privileged to accompany hundreds of people as they leave behind the norms of ordinary life in search of the "something more" they long for. And what we discover as we journey together is always far more than what we could ever imagine alone.

**Pilgrims and Sojourners**

Every religious tradition has sacred spaces that commemorate special moments of encounter with the divine. We call the people who go to them pilgrims. But we are all searching for meaning. We want coherence and order, even as we often need to disrupt the ordinary and mundane in order to re-connect with what matters to us. In so far as each one of us hungers for something more, we are all pilgrims.

But pilgrimages are temporary. They ask us to suspend our ordinary habits and leave behind what is familiar to us in order



*Gillian T.W. Ahlgren*

to be given new insights and perspectives. Pilgrimages can be intense experiences, with sensory and experiential dimensions that capture our imaginations. They exist in a particular moment of time and space in order to pierce us with some sense of the sacred.   Pilgrimages are different from the ways that we more routinely journey together as sojourners on a common path to reclaim human goodness and be instruments of peace, light and hope in a troubled world.

Pilgrimages are not intended to be sustainable, particularly in their intensity.  Yet I cannot believe that they are meant to exist as "peak experiences," unrepeatable and otherworldly. Pilgrimage is not intended to help us escape from life; pilgrimage is a special, temporary time meant to help us re-imagine ourselves and our world, so that we live in greater integrity and collaboration with the divine and with one another.  The challenge, for all people of faith, is to integrate into daily life the insights, experiences and lessons learned in such suspended times, so that we are continually growing together in a deepening commitment to a better world.

I stumbled, alone and inadvertently, into my first pilgrimage when I went to Europe for the first time at the age of 19.  In fact, I became a church historian and theologian in large part because of that journey.  Given an extra ticket on an excursion to the Benedictine monastery of Montserrat, a revered space of natural beauty for the Catalan people, I looked up at the serrated mountains above the monastic complex and felt somehow a part of something much greater than myself. What would motivate a person to join a monastic community, I wondered, and what did its members think they were accomplishing? The same curiosity and wonder came to me a few weeks later, as I circled very slowly around the choir of the cathedral of Chartres, gazing at scene after scene of the life of Christ, illuminated by the colored light of sunshine streaming through stained glass windows.  Why would a whole city devote its intellectual, artistic, technological, economic and human resources toward the construction of a cathedral?  I found myself filled with questions about human motivation and aspiration, especially whether or not (and how), as humans, we come to know God.

Upon my return to the U.S., those questions were greeted with encouragement both by professors who mentored me and friends who explored them with me. They led me to doctoral work in the history of Christianity and in the Christian mystical tradition. As I studied and learned about a tradition of sojourning people, past and present, who asked the deepest questions that human beings can ask, I have sought to share those questions with others.  Year after year, the journey continues, inside university classrooms, with pastoral workers in the community, and in the footsteps of some of Christianity's greatest visionary thinkers.

One of the great constants, since 1999, has been the Spiritual Immersion Experiences in the footsteps of Francis and Clare that I facilitate.  Each time I go, I am privileged to watch people fall in love—with life and, often, with God.  Experiencing together Francis and Clare's simplicity and sincerity helps all of us to fall in love with the goodness of life.  Over the years, I have seen how our experiences of walking together in intentional community can help people negotiate significant challenges with deeper grace and energy, can renew love relationships, and can provide people with the inspiration and strength to change careers or make other critical life decisions.

It does not necessarily take engaging a physical pilgrimage to find meaning or to fall in love with God.  But it does take leaving behind, in some significant way, the self that we have constructed up to any given moment, so that we can be touched by God in new ways.  Whether as pilgrims or sojourners, our



*Gillian T.W. Ahlgren*

work is always to wean ourselves from personal and social markers of identity, choosing instead to define ourselves as being on a lifelong journey to reclaim our souls and our humanity. It is the "going out" of the smallness of ourselves that is critical. Indeed, if we are not willing to leave behind elements of the self and the smallness of our own perspectives in order to grow and be changed, we will never truly engage pilgrimage or the spiritual life, no matter how far we travel.

If we want to find the love that gives meaning to our lives, we must own a process of inquiry, exploration, and change. The first step in finding what we want is to actively seek it. This requires us to go outside the self. Ironically, in the life of the Spirit, it takes leaving the self to actually find the self. A common refrain within mystical texts is that our search for God is, at the same time, a search for our authentic selves. The fundamental hypothesis in this search—one that is confirmed after we have first taken the risk of testing it in our own experience—is that we are created for relationship, with God and one another. This is not simply a "faith statement;" it is a premise about our humanity that each of us, for our own well-being, needs to test and explore in the laboratory of life. The journey toward our authentic humanity is a communal one, and God reveals Godself to us in new and surprising ways as we seek God's presence in our own lived experience. If "the Lord your God is in your midst," as the prophet Zephaniah (3:17) asserted, we need one another to discover that reality.


**Journeying Together**

The life of Jesus as it is portrayed in the gospels manifests love in action. In Mark, for example, Jesus is portrayed as moving throughout Galilee, teaching and healing, surrounded by companions, and constantly in contact with people. Early on, this same lifestyle of journeying "two by two… taking nothing for the journey" (Mark 6:7-8) became the norm for Jesus's companions, who went forth to share healing and hope, in imitation of what they themselves had been learning. Women and men gave voice to what they had experienced through their contact with Jesus; this work of "missionary discipleship" is a vocation shared by all who call themselves Christian. The Samaritan woman who conversed with Jesus at Jacob's well drew many Samaritans toward Jesus, and they first came to believe in him "because of the woman's testimony." (John 4:39) Conversion and transformation happen through the lived experience of God in our midst, just as the earliest disciples realized on the road to Emmaus. As they reflected together and remembered, they recognized the life and meaning they were finding in their shared journey toward deeper authenticity and love: Were not our hearts burning within us? The first several chapters of Acts reflect this model of a community in constant action: men and women, gathered and going forth, sharing their possessions and bearing witness, in word and in deed, to the love of God.

1200 years later, the early Christian model of simplicity and purpose struck a deep chord in the heart of a young war veteran from Assisi struggling to make sense of the human spirit. Sources describe how Francis felt liberated for action when he heard particular passages from scripture, which he received joyfully as instructions for his new form of life:

When he heard that Christ's disciples should not possess gold or silver or money, or carry on their journey a wallet or a sack, nor bread nor a staff, nor to have shoes nor two tunics, but that they should preach the reign of God and reconciliation, the holy man Francis, immediately exulted in the spirit of God. "This is what I want!" he said. "This is what I seek, this is what I desire with all my heart." Overflowing

                                    *Gillian T.W. Ahlgren*

with joy, Francis hastened to implement the words… and was careful to carry them out to the letter. (Thomas of Celano, *The Life of St. Francis*, 1:9:22, in Armstrong et al., *The Saint*, 201-2.)

Francis wanted to model the simplicity of spirit and genuine human warmth that Jesus taught, knowing that people needed to see human goodness in action if they were going to trust that a more humane and generous way of living was truly possible.

The framework of "walking with one another in the presence of God" is what best characterizes this way of proceeding, as companions to one another along the way. Companions share bread together; this is the literal meaning of the word "companion." In English, we derive the word "accompaniment" from the same root as "companions," and it points to our willingness to walk with and accompany others through all the phases and challenges of their lives. When we break bread together, we share with one another what we have, but, more importantly, we share who we are. And all of us emerge the richer, the wiser, and the more empowered for it.

Likewise, the journey to discover the God in our midst is concurrently one of self-sharing. On the journey, we share our stories. In the safety of a caring community, we confide our questions, our doubts, and our dreams. We receive encouragement in our growth, insights from others, and, most importantly, we come to understand that we are never alone on the way. "Accompaniment" is the common ground between pilgrims and sojourners, and as we accompany one another we learn how to share life together in ways that reveal the God who is known in our midst.

Humbly and with great vision and hope, Pope Francis, centuries later, urged *all of us* to learn anew "the art of accompaniment" which teaches us

> to remove our sandals before the sacred ground of the other (cf. Exodus 3:5). The pace of this accompaniment must be steady and reassuring, reflecting our closeness and our compassionate gaze which also heals, liberates and encourages growth in the Christian life. (Pope Francis, *Joy of the Gospel*, par. 169)

Genuine accompaniment always adds meaning to our lives. For accompaniment is *both* the way of the gospel *and* the best way of being human. When our questions, our doubts, and our struggles are acknowledged and honored by those around us, we realize that we are courageously moving toward greater and greater authenticity. When our gifts, our insights, and our growth are affirmed, we see ourselves making progress toward the persons we strive to be. The suggestion here is that genuine accompaniment, like genuine pilgrimage, brings a helpful and productive fruitfulness to our lives. We find happiness and fulfillment through journeying together because we gain clarity about the meaning and purpose of our lives as we share with others what is meaningfully unique about us—what we were brought into this world to share with others. Sharing the journey gives us deeper insight into who we are meant to be.

We are constantly learning who we are in light of the relationships that form our being. Opening ourselves to the ways in which God's presence, in us and in our world, provides orientation, purpose and meaning to our own presence here on earth. Nurturing intentional relationship with God, allowing God to reveal Godself to us in ever new ways and in the ways that God chooses is surprising and revelatory—the fundamental journey of our human existence. The many ways that God illuminates our understanding can peck away at whatever deception we are currently laboring under—if we let it. With clarity and compassion, the tender touch of the divine hand indicates all spaces where we need to grow and makes clear the many ways that our actions contradict God's loving intent for us and for our world. Our willingness to respond to God's constant encouragement to grow toward greater integrity then invites us to embody, all the more thoroughly, God's loving vision of justice, dignity and fullness of life for all.

We have all heard of "the teachable moment," in a classroom or even in a family conversation, when something happens or something is said that creates an opportunity to examine or explore our experience and learn something profound from it. To live our lives in such a constantly teachable way, always willing to learn something new and grow in response to what we learn, reflects our growing sensitivity to the movements of the Spirit, in ourselves and in our world, as well as a deepening commitment and attunement to the invitation of God in every moment. What a relief to know that "God's presence accompanies the sincere efforts of individuals and groups to find encouragement and meaning in their lives." (See Pope Francis, *Joy of the Gospel*, par. 71)

There is something sacred about our walking together, for in sincere togetherness we create new paths. Indeed, it is in taking the risk to set out on a journey with others, in search of the Something More that we long for, that life really begins.

**FOR REFLECTION:**

Choose a passage from the chapter that rang true to you from your own experience. Explore how the particulars of your experience might amplify or change the passage.

What price do we pay as human beings if we ignore our desire for greater meaning?

What is the working definition of spirituality implicit in this chapter? What are some of the challenges inherent in defining spirituality?

What benefits do you see in cultivating a personal spirituality? What roles do companions and community play in that process?

**2**

# The Need for Meaning:
# What Will We Do with Our Discontent?

While it is possible for us to find the goodness, love, and meaning we most deeply desire, we live in a world oriented toward competition, superficiality, indifference, and even violence—forces that can splinter us within and disconnect us from one another. Is it any wonder that we feel in our hearts, our psyches and our very bones the many contradictions of being human?

But what if dissatisfaction and disillusionment, as disorienting as they can be, are actually spiritual indicators of our own need for radical change? Can confusion and even distress, when addressed honestly and within safe relational contexts, invite us into a search that ultimately brings us to new life?

Often when we think of great spiritual leaders of the past, we forget that they, too, had to confront great social and psychological darkness as they grew toward personal integrity and deepening relationship with God and others. In this chapter I would like to look carefully at the early life narratives of Francis and Clare, so that we can read them as mirrors into our own struggles for integrity. Their early years of doubt, confusion, and searching provided them with a deep strength to say no to what was death-dealing about their world. By rejecting norms and paradigms that did not support their dignity, integrity or goodness, they teach us that the only way forward lies in being deeply honest about what is not working, in our own lives and in the world around us.

Francis and Clare found strength and resolve through the rawness of their early lives. Each was propelled toward a deep search for meaning as a direct result of human violence. For Francis, it was injury during a battle at Collestrada, where, at the age of 20, he lay wounded and might have been left to die. But his Perugian enemies recognized in Francis's suit of armor the potential value he had in captivity.

Francis's experience as a prisoner of war taught him early on the double edge of wealth and power. His vulnerability during that painful year allowed him to see that, in his own ways, he had participated in the same habits of exploitation, vendetta and violence that had left him alone and abandoned. Ransomed and returned back to his family in 1203, Francis found himself unable to reintegrate back into the same society that had sent him into battle. Rather, he began to see that continuing with business as usual was actually a slow form of death, and he grew daily more convinced that there had to be a different, better way.

Clare, too, was deeply impacted by the violence embedded in both her family system and in the larger culture. A child caught up in the civil war in Assisi, she was forced to seek political asylum and spent years of her childhood as a refugee, ironically in Perugia as well. Observing the impact of war on her society, she refused to perpetuate its patriarchal assumptions and then faced strong resistance when she rejected them and refused to marry. She dedicated her life to forming and nurturing a vision of love that created viable alternatives for women and men, rooted in dignity, respect and mutuality.



*Gillian T.W. Ahlgren*

Over the course of the next two chapters, we will explore the profoundly disruptive impact that violence had in the lives of Francis and Clare as young people. This will help us to understand the urgency of their search for personal meaning, their decisive rejection of many of the norms of their culture, and their capacity to recognize early on in their lives all that is at stake in the values that our communities embody. One of their greatest contributions, both to their own contemporaries and to us today, is the depth of their desire to create a community of mutual belonging—a community in which every person matters and has a part to play in making our world a home for all. If we explore how they responded to the human hunger to belong and to be of service to something bigger than ourselves, we might discover that we, too, have similar desires. We will trace each of their stories separately, recognizing their growing influence on each other but allowing their very different backgrounds and struggles to speak independently. I explore their early experience in detail, because the context of profound transition in which they lived has so many parallels to our own historical moment right now.

Pope Francis identified our time as "a turning point in history," asking us

> ...to remember that the majority of our contemporaries are barely living from day to day, with dire consequences. A number of diseases are spreading. The hearts of many people are gripped by fear and desperation, even in the so-called rich countries. The joy of living frequently fades, lack of respect for others and violence are on the rise, and inequality is increasingly evident. It is a struggle to live and, often, to live with precious little dignity. This epochal change has been set in motion by the enormous qualitative, quantitative, rapid and cumulative advances occurring in the sciences and in technology, and by their instant application

in different areas of nature and of life. We are in an age of knowledge and information, which has led to new and often anonymous kinds of power. (Pope Francis, *Joy of the Gospel*, par. 52)

It is a system, Pope Francis states, "where the powerful feed upon the powerless," and "human beings are themselves considered consumer goods to be used and then discarded. We have created a 'disposable' culture which is now spreading," a culture of prosperity that deadens us and is sustained by the "globalization of indifference." (See Pope Francis, *Joy of the Gospel*, pars. 53-4)

In direct contrast, Francis and Clare remind us that we are not meant to adjust to dehumanization. We have an intuitive capacity to recognize things that, at the human level, are simply wrong and compromise our humanity. This sensitivity to pathologies within our own cultures and communities is a positive human instinct that must be cultivated for our own well-being.

Francis and Clare, too, lived in a historical moment of great turbulence and change. Small cities like theirs were the nerve centers of a massive transition from a land-based feudal economic system to the commercial revolution of the thirteenth century. Assisi is perched on a hilltop where it could be defended from external attack and where citizens, safely ensconced within the city walls, could pursue their private and collective socio-economic interests. Assisi's success as a city depended on the rise of the merchant class, in a painful and conflictive transition that provoked civic unrest and even war between nearby cities.

The very topography of Assisi tells this story. The Piazza del Commune is the heart of the city, and streets radiate out of it like living limbs. The piazza served as a midway point between the palazzos of the nobility and the living quarters and shops of the merchant and working classes below them. Up a steep hill east of the piazza is the church of San Rufino. Clare's noble family owned the building adjoining the church; a notarized document of 1148 shows her grandfather's pledge not to enlarge the family palace if it would interfere with the cathedral's façade. Several levels below Clare's home was the household of the Bernardone family.

Francis's father Pietro di Bernardone was a powerful and influential man, although his status was constantly shadowed by the fact that he had acquired his wealth as a cloth merchant, rather than having inherited his money and, more importantly his social position, as a member of the noble class would have. Pietro was a shrewd and ambitious businessman, and, as he acquired more and more wealth, he sought to purchase land in the valley below the city. In centuries past, feudal norms would have made such aspirations impossible. But times were changing. Taking advantage of many years of drought and famine toward the end of the twelfth century, Pietro bought up tracts from struggling noble families who had to liquidate their assets when the real estate failed to produce income. Pietro was therefore what used to be called nouveau riche, and his son Francis spent the family's disposable income freely. Today we might call this conspicuous consumption, a practice designed to trumpet the family's growing economic power. Early sources sometimes describe Francis as being subject to the vanity of the age. Yet they are also quick to point out that even as a youth Francis was more characterized by generosity than greed. For example, early biographer Thomas of Celano writes: "Since he was very rich, he was not greedy but extravagant, not a hoarder of money but a squanderer of his property, a prudent dealer but a most unreliable steward." Francis appears to have been a popular young man of charm, wit, good humor, and the prodigal generosity of a spoiled son whose joyful, free spirit delighted in music and revelry of all sorts.

At the age of fifteen, Francis was considered a man, able to enter apprenticeship and capable of bearing arms. He began to accompany his father on the annual trip to Troyes to learn the logistics of the family business. The men took goods with them to sell and purchased silk fabrics from the east that came into port cities like Genoa and Venice. Damasks, brocades, embossed silks and satin; over the years Pietro had acquired a keen sense of market demand and was eager to teach Francis the secrets of the trade. The fair at Troyes also exposed Francis to Provençal culture—the troubadour tradition with its ideals of chivalry and courtly love—all things that he had shared with his mother in his earliest years of childhood education. The knightly ideals of this tradition fed and romanticized the exploits of war, but Francis also saw, in his travels, real violence—brawls, the threat of thieves on the long journey, and the need for weapons to protect property. Whether on the road or in the fair's encampments, Francis could hardly have been unaware of an entire network of unsavory characters ranging from thieves and moneychangers to pimps and prostitutes. Even safely home in Assisi, a great deal of violence and sexual licentiousness, often ritualized in festivals, prevailed. Francis's privileged position enabled him to participate as he liked, funding parties and squandering his wealth on things the he later would find sad and even repugnant.

Clare, on the other hand, was described universally by her peers as being one of the most upright and compassionate of Christian women, even before she entered religious life. Clare's graces and virtues consisted of her "great honesty, kindness, and humility," and witnesses at her canonization process testified repeatedly to her generosity to the poor. Not only was she described as distributing food and alms, she also tried to give away her dowry, having decided that she would not marry but would instead consecrate herself to God. Those who saw her way of life from within the cloister said just about to a person, that they could not even find words to describe her holiness. (These testimonies are collected in *Clare: The Lady* in the bibliography below.)

Francis and Clare could hardly have come from more different social circumstances: Clare came from an influential noble household; her family's palace was located in one of the most prestigious sections of the city. Francis's family was heavily invested in overturning the traditional political dominance of the nobility in local governance. Throughout Italy, the shift from a feudal economy to a monetary-based, urban economy involved massive changes in the political, social and religious landscape. Tensions rooted in this fundamental shift in the economic base were made even more complex because they were not just economic. They also depended upon the loyalties of individual cities either to the pope or to the Holy Roman Emperor. In the region of Umbria, the cities of Assisi, Rieti, Spoleto, Foligno, and Nocera were governed by the emperor's representative Conrad, which set them against their neighbor Perugia, which had pledged itself to the papacy.

The imposing Rocca Maggiore, a fortress dominating the hilltop over Assisi, symbolizes the struggle. Technically, Rocca Maggiore was the permanent residence of Conrad, the powerful Duke of Spoleto, who kept a garrison of guards there and was able to host Emperor Henry VI the few times that he visited. Practically, the fortress served to protect those few allowed into it, during times of social unrest or attack by hostile forces. In 1198, when Francis was about 16 years old and Clare perhaps 5, the merchant class assembled an attack on the upper section of the city inhabited by the nobles. They hoped to establish Assisi as its own *comune*, with new governing ordinances that would allow greater property rights for all. Taking advantage of a moment when Conrad was away negotiating with papal representatives, they attacked and destroyed the residence. Francis may have participated in this attack, which successfully dismantled imperial power and established a new city government. We know that Francis's father Pietro had invested heavily in this attack because he is listed in state archives as a financial backer and benefactor of the communal state.

The uprising of Assisi's merchant class sent much of the nobility, including Clare and her family, to Perugia to seek asylum. Assisi's exiled nobles aligned themselves with the city of Perugia, a historic rival of Assisi, and together they prepared to take back the city. Four years of civil war erupted, and Francis's early adulthood was marked by repeated calls to arms in battles across the Spoleto valley. Towers and fortresses were taken down; properties were trampled and destroyed. No one invested in the fertile valley could sit back and let the savage Perugian attacks go unchecked. Francis's father invested money in armor for Francis, who then prepared, with the other young men of Assisi, to go to war. Defense of the city would have been considered their civic duty, and it would have come with the blessing of the local bishop.

Francis found himself in the elite Compagnia dei Cavalieri, when, in 1202, he was struck down and injured. His armor informed his captors of the wealth of his family and therefore saved his life; Francis was dragged through the streets of Perugia and thrown into prison until his family offered a suitable ransom for his return. Negotiations for such an outcome took time, and Francis languished for nearly a year in captivity. Although we know very little about this time in his life, we can easily imagine the challenges, to both body and soul, caused by confinement, injury, illness, and a host of uncertainties about his future. Being imprisoned in Perugia was deeply formative for Francis, causing him to question the social and religious values and assumptions that had led him to such ignominious circumstances.



*Gillian T.W. Ahlgren*

In her own way, Clare, too, was learning how the social codes of the day prevented her from developing in her own right. Ironically, throughout Francis's entire time in Perugia as a prisoner of war, Clare was also there, her family still displaced after the class struggles in Assisi. During her early years, Clare's male relatives were often absent from the household, defending the family's interests in battle and leaving domestic matters primarily in the hands of Clare's mother. In 1202, during Francis's year of imprisonment in Perugia, Clare would have been nine years old, and she was now being actively prepared for marriage and household management. She learned from her mother practical skills of reading, penmanship, and needlepoint. Yet she also observed the tremendous cost to women of the violence of the time: they had to oversee large properties on their own, they were the ones to nurse the men back to health after being wounded in battle, and, without having had any say in the matter, they were often thrown into precarious, even volatile circumstances through widowhood or their family members' incapacitation. The conflicting values of her culture could not have been clearer to Clare, for her mother was devout and very committed to spiritual practices of kindness, generosity, prayer, and pilgrimages to holy places, including visits to Rome and Jerusalem. Both Francis and Clare, then, were poised to question the assumptions of a culture of war and privilege, based on their own deeply personal observations of its cost to the human spirit.

Francis returned to Assisi dazed and disoriented after his year of imprisonment in Perugia. In taking up arms and defending his city, he had, according to all the standards of his day, made the right civic, moral, even religious decision. He had conducted himself with honor, both in battle and during his imprisonment, and yet he had suffered confinement, indignity, and the distress of not knowing when, even if, he would be released to his family. Although historical sources say almost nothing about this time in Francis's life—only that he suffered grave illness—we can imagine that the dank cells, miserable food and poor sanitation likely provoked dysentery, fever, and other disease. When he finally did return to Assisi, in late 1203, Francis was physically weakened and gravely disoriented. His earliest biographer, Thomas of Celano, records that he was "worn down by his long illness" and hobbled about with a cane when he was finally able to get out of bed. It is hard to know what these experiences did to Francis's spirit, inside and out. Certainly, they had exposed him to violence, pettiness, cruelty, callousness and any number of indignities from which his wealth and social status had previously insulated him. His vulnerability forced him to examine and re-assess the values and assumptions of his time and culture.

Before his capture, Francis looked ahead to a future that was his for the taking: successful management of his father's cloth business, perhaps even a celebrated marriage into a noble family—in short, a long and happy continuation of all that he had known as the cherished son of one of Assisi's notable, up-and-coming families. For a young man of a prosperous family who was accustomed to autonomy and a carefree lifestyle, imprisonment, illness, confinement and powerlessness were radically new experiences. Alone, ill, hungry, and abused, Francis experienced a humbling vulnerability that ultimately proved invaluable to his appreciation of the holy fragility of life itself. A profound inner shift had occurred over the course of his year in Perugia, and that shift became apparent only upon his return to Assisi. Even the loving care of his mother could not restore the happy-go-lucky youth who had gone off to war. His old habits, patterns and values ceased to hold any meaning for him. Imprisonment had shattered his casual, privileged view of life, and he found himself both unwilling and unable to return to business as usual.

*　*　*



*Gillian T.W. Ahlgren*

*In Assisi we retrace this moment in Francis's life on the second day of our immersion in the footsteps of Francis and Clare. We head to the top of the city of Perugia, set high on a hill, and, as we take in details of the beautiful 15th-century facades, the group is completely unaware that the streets we are walking on have been laid out over the city's intact medieval foundation. Like most European cities, modern Perugia was built on top of medieval Perugia, and this phenomenon is experienced in a rather exceptional way there. The labyrinth of medieval ramparts and passageways has been preserved and renovated with the inclusion of a complex set of "scala mobile," or escalators. This juxtaposition of modern and medieval is fascinating to experience in its own right, but we do this in a way that emphasizes the social disparities that Francis and Clare were themselves becoming aware of.*

*First, we head down the streets of the modern city toward the Galleria Nazionale, where an astonishing collection of Umbrian art awaits us. It is like stepping into the history of Christian art. We spend nearly three hours contemplating the humanity of Christ as it gradually becomes more and more subtle, alive, and beautiful over the course of the centuries. We see the body of Christ on the cross taking form and shape and becoming deeply human, deeply real—no longer soaring absently over suffering, in the "Christ the victor" pose. Gradually, the body gains weight and gravity, pulled down by sin, and the self-offering of Christ becomes clearer, as in a one-of-a-kind image of Christ reaching out, leaning down toward the world with an open-armed embrace. The image is so real that, if you didn't have the curator's word for it being a mid-thirteenth-century rendition, you might wonder (as I did when I first saw it), why the museum had put a modern crucifix up in the middle of a room full of medieval ones. In this* **Cristo deposto***, ostensibly an image of Christ being taken down from the cross, Christ is still caught in the pose of the cross, but his arms are not nailed. Instead they have fallen forward in a gentle, tender embrace toward the world. His eyes are closed, but even his face is tender. The outstretched arms of Christ appear in such* *a spontaneous, loving gesture, free from the details of suffering that appear on the other thirteenth-century crucifixes, that the contrast—like the blazing love of God itself—is almost shocking. But perhaps in this simple, piercing cross, we are given a privileged glimpse of the lenses with which Francis and Clare saw Christ and saw the world: always, always through the eyes of love. We continue around the room, watching the crucifixion take on sharper dimensions, begging us, as viewers, to feel compassion, pity, sorrow, and connection.*

*We move onto room after room of Madonna and Childs, watching their relationship come alive, Mary gradually ceasing to be a wooden-like "throne" for the miniature adult Christ on her knee, and coming into herself, her humanity, her beauty, her maternity, her joy, with wonderful details of the intimacy of mother and child working their way into the images as the decades spill on. We watch their gracious affection with one another as a real baby grasps at his mother's finger or nurses gratefully at her breast. We see the tilt of their heads toward us, the viewers, trying to draw us into the same intimacy with God and with the holy in our own lives. These are the kinds of things I spend thousands of words trying to communicate in a classroom: what does it mean for us to affirm that God became truly and fully human? And the aha moment as the reality of the incarnation comes alive so clearly for people is glorious indeed. Finally, as we work our way through scene after scene, we see Francis and Clare take their place in the communion of saints, and the visual feast invites us to take more seriously, as a prayerful practice, the art of gazing and beholding, of reflection and contemplation.*

*It is usually about 5:00 or so when we pour, sated, out of the museum in search of a cappuccino and conversation. And even this dimension of our experience in Perugia is à propos. Perugia was known, in its time, for being a flashy city with an opulent lifestyle—full of wealth, with a propensity toward violence both to defend its wealth and, simply, as a way of life. In our own small way we experience the careless extravagance, even hard-hearted blindness as we sit above the bowels of the city, sipping, snacking, and people-watching.*

　　　　　　　　　　　　　　　　*Gillian T.W. Ahlgren*

*But young Francis did not experience Perugia in this privileged way. The Perugians were his sworn enemies, determined to take over Assisi, and Francis rode off, innocently enough, to defend his home and his family and his people, only to be captured and imprisoned and suffer malaria and dysentery and God knows what else in the confines of prison. Everything—his dreams, his cherished ideals, his future—came tumbling down in a mass of misery there, and this becomes quite easy for us to imagine as we finish our coffees and continue our tour of the city. Now we descend down a long set of escalators, underneath the actual city streets, and enter a labyrinth of dark medieval passageways with gated cells on either side. We spend about twenty minutes walking in deliberate silence together, engaging in a walking meditation, pausing in front of a locked cell or two to contemplate the wretchedness that is also, so often, a hidden and repressed part of the human experience, forced down into the darkness below the superficial gaiety of the world above.*

*We leave Perugia with a strong sense of that poignant space that is, paradoxically, both our wounded, human vulnerability and our strength—our openness to God and to all that we trust God can and will work within us. And we reflect on the "gift of tears" described in our readings for the day—what Alan Jones, in* **Soul Making: The Desert Way of Spirituality**, *calls the tears that flow "when the real source of our life is uncovered, when the mask of pretense is dropped, when our strategies of self-deception are abandoned." Such tears, Jones says, come "when we learn to live more and more out of our deepest longings, our needs, our troubles. These must all surface and be given their rightful place. For in them we find our real human life in all its depths." (Alan Jones,* **Soul Making: The Desert Way of Spirituality**, *p. 83)*

*   *   *

Francis's early biographers do not mention his experience as a prisoner of war. They seem completely unaware of its impact on him. Perhaps this should not surprise us, for we are only very recently in our human history coming to terms with the long-term effects of war, on us and on our children. As the technology of war has gotten both far more sophisticated and far more sinister, we cannot afford to be naïve or self-deceptive about its impact, on us and on our world. The economic cost of war has brought about global economic and social instability as governments scramble to pay for it, and the human cost is seen in a global crisis of displacement, refugees, and generational instability that is completely unsustainable.

Surely Francis would want us to take a careful and thorough look at what has become normative in our world and to question if this is truly what we want, for ourselves and for our children. This search for a more just, more humane way of life is precisely what he modeled for his own contemporaries, after the tragedy and senselessness of war "awakened" the intense thirst of his spirit for genuine peace. Slowly, this thirst opened his eyes to a new and painful comprehension of the interlocking forces of power—economic, political, and social—that drove the violence and warfare of his day.

For Francis, the basic problem was lodged in the prevailing cultural assumption that acquiring property, and defending it when necessary, was morally neutral. This assumption bred a culture that routinely used violence when defending its economic or politic interests, and church officials did nothing substantive to challenge this pattern. Bishops and popes brokered relations with political forces and then blessed young people as they went off to war in defense of economic and political interests.

As the dissonances of his culture grew intolerable, Francis felt an intensifying need to say "no." No to the violence. No to the

                                        *Gillian T.W. Ahlgren*

status quo. Francis's way of being creatively and courageously faithful in his day and age was not an easy way. But to him and to others it felt both necessary and freeing. This kind of honesty about what mattered to him and what moved him led to a deepening orientation to God—a God who was asking Francis to choose life, not death, for himself and for others.

As part of our walk in Francis's footsteps, perhaps we could look, for a moment, at our own world, through his eyes. Ignatius Loyola, founder of the Jesuits, would call this consideration an "examen"—an examination of conscience and consciousness—and it is a process that we engage as we examine our own conduct and as we examine the assumptions of the communities and societies within which we live. Like Francis, Ignatius was moved toward this prayerful consideration of his life, as well as how the assumptions of his culture and society had conditioned him to see reality, as he, too, recovered from the impact of war. In many ways, Pope Francis, the world's first Jesuit pope, modeled the social dimensions of this Ignatian practice as an intentional, daily practice. It is in this Ignatian tradition of taking a "long, loving look at the real" (a phrase coined by Jesuit Walter Burghardt) that we conclude this chapter by turning from Francis's context to the historical reality of our day. But where to begin? For violence is at least as culturally, even globally, embedded in our current reality as it was in Francis's own.

We could begin by noticing the sheer scope of the problem. It might not surprise us to realize that we have grown more violent in modern times, rather than less so, and that civilians continue to suffer, in even higher numbers than active combatants. Historians estimate, for example, that in the wars of the twentieth century not less than 62 million civilians were killed, nearly 20 million more than the 43 million military personnel killed. While it is too early in the twenty-first century to compare, we can easily see that the first two decades suggest an era of even more violence and trauma.  In fact, much of what we see shows a complete obliteration of life. The sophistication of war technology does not keep us from protecting civilians from its ravages.  In fact, as the technology of war has grown more sophisticated and more profitable, it has claimed more of our infrastructures, embedded its way into our global economic fabric, and become nearly ubiquitous.

Also disturbing is how insidious war has become.  What we call "the defense industry" is a powerful economic force, far surpassing the capacity of judicial systems and international organizations to monitor and intervene when human rights and international law are violated. Further, war has become privatized in ways that disrupt the relationship between combatants and the traditional civil and military codes that attempt to provide behavioral parameters or disciplinary consequences for soldiers. War can be and is waged on far more fronts than we recognize— information systems, deprivation of food, power grids, banking networks, enslavement of peoples—and its tentacles suck out resources that our children and our earth desperately need.

War correspondent Chris Hedges has notably described war as the "force that gives us meaning."  Its lethal seduction lies in its capacity to give people a cause, an identity, and a resolve that they might otherwise not be able to find on their own. In the absence of cultural, communal, and spiritual meaning, war serves as a potent and corrosive default.  For the young in particular, military service can be an important source of identity: "Many of us, restless and unfulfilled, see no supreme worth in our lives. We want more out of life.  And war, at least, gives us a sense that we can rise above our smallness." But, as Hedges warns, engaging in warfare tends to generate a toxic culture, as war "distorts memory, corrupts language, and infects everything around it…. War makes the world understandable, a black and white tableau of them and us.  It suspends thought, especially self-critical thought."  (See Chris Hedges, *War as a Force for Meaning*, pp. 3, 7, 10)  A community, nation or culture that invests its resources in violence easily loses humane habits of creatively sharing ideas, collaborative problem solving, and envisioning social and global well-being.

Once war has been declared and often long before it is official, the industries that profit from it and the mindsets that support it are stronger and more pervasive than we acknowledge. Violence becomes a cultural norm and begins to displace creative alternatives within the human community.  We fold violence into our belief systems, and its tentacles encompass our values, squeezing the life out of them.  As violence becomes more normalized, it also becomes more entrenched, and we tend to deny its lethal impact on all of us.  Often it is the testimonies of those who have suffered its impact—surviving civilians and even some veterans—who can call us back to our senses, if we listen to their voices.  Such prophets remind us that no human community survives war unscathed.  Violence perpetuates and feeds the annihilation of all of us.  Apart from the immediate social, environmental, and economic damage it wreaks, violence turns us into servants of a system that disconnects us from our well-being and even our humanity.

The violence insidious in our world today encompasses many forms, from outright war zones to kidnapping, organized crime, human trafficking, slavery and sexual exploitation.  As we reflect on these early years in the lives of Francis and Clare, we see that they were no strangers to such harsh realities.  The lens of contemporary psychology helps us identify the trauma of war on both of them—on Francis as a combatant and on Clare as a civilian refugee.  As a former veteran explains to my "St. Francis and Pope Francis" seminar students when he comes into class to reflect with us: "After war there is no 'reintegration'.  When you have been changed by trauma and war, you do not neatly fit back into a social structure that increasingly raises questions for you about what matters."

In the immediate aftermath of such experiences, there may not be clarity about what matters or where to find meaning, healing or coherence, but there is at least the undeniable knowledge that we have been changed—and not necessarily for the better. We have been put radically in touch with forces of malice and destruction. We may have participated in and collaborated with such forces—wholeheartedly or less willingly. Or it may have cost us all that we had to have resisted or survived them. Wherever on that spectrum that we find ourselves, we must now live with the consequences of what we have lived through.

The result is often some form or another of rupture, even alienation, from self, family and/or society. In domestic and relational experiences of violence, where the violence is more chronic than merely situational, the interior damage can be even more difficult to sort out, as the forces that have torn us apart are closer to home and may even have been difficult or impossible to avoid. Individuals who were supposed to be colleagues, friends, or family (and therefore who were supposed to treat us with respect, care, and even cherishing) have violated our trust, piercing a hole in the trustworthiness of our beliefs, our hopes, our investments of time, treasure, allegiance and affect.

To recover from this wounding takes time, energy and relational support. And in the aftermath of such eye-opening experiences, everything becomes subject to greater scrutiny in order to assess its veracity, its authenticity, and its trustworthiness, so that we can consider the authority it should (or should not) have over us. But, as Judith Herman observes, "Remembering and telling the truth about terrible events are prerequisites for the restoration of social order and for the healing of individual victims," even as it is difficult to "find a language that conveys fully and persuasively what one has seen." (See Judith Herman, *Trauma and Recovery*, pp. 1-2)

The struggle for meaning and coherence after trauma has the gift of exposing incoherence and inauthenticity, and it has, in some, ironically, been the seed toward the slow and prophetic work of integrating our deepest principles and values into our personal and social actions. When we recognize that we have suffered moral injury and that our society, culture, family or institutions either do not recognize the injustice or are even perpetuating it, our opened eyes are hard to close, even though the temptation to sleepwalk through life can be intense. Our own personal sensitization to the existence of lethal forces, however, can give us a prophetic way to probe the roots of toxicity and see the many ways that it wears down the human community, deadening us to our goodness, as we become complicit in actions, movements, and cultural norms that violate us or others. If we commit ourselves to a more rigorous and truthful way of understanding our reality, prophetic voices are born.

Francis does not talk about the questions he carried in his heart after Perugia, so there is nothing we can know with certainty about his first year back in Assisi after his imprisonment. All we know is that he could not and would not go back to business as usual. We certainly can postulate that Francis had been given new eyes with which to see his own community. He must have made the causal connection between property ownership and the apparent need to defend property. And he must have begun to question whether or not anyone, including himself and his family members, had a right to luxury items when some people did not have enough to feed their own families.

We will explore the steps of the slow change in his perspectives and the courage and commitments he gained as he underwent a process of deep change in the next chapter.  For now, it is enough for us to imagine Francis's kind, questioning, newly-opened eyes as he began to want a world where people were safe, where children were fed, where no one was subject to war, violence, imprisonment, and exploitation.  It is enough to allow those eyes to help us ask the questions that our world needs us to be asking—simple questions with simple answers that, once answered will require great changes of us.  Do we really want to purchase products made by children who should be in school?  Do we really want to be dependent upon fossil fuels that rob us and the next generation of the clean air, clean water and healthy earth that all of us need?  Do we really prefer styrofoam cups and single-use plastics to glaciers and tropical rainforests?  Do we really prefer hand-wringing over the loss of species of plants and animals to the changes necessary to preserve biodiversity and ecosystems?  Do we really think that we can continue "business as usual" on this hurting planet?  Will we live with our eyes closed or open?

If we are truly going to journey toward authenticity, integrity and well-being, then we will need courage to confront deception and to find our deepest truths.  In the face of troubling awarenesses, the temptation to avoid, deny, or "move on" is even stronger.  But if we are courageous enough to seek the truth of our lives and to press on for meaning in the face of meaninglessness, our own disillusionment can help us break through the layers of deception that surround us.  Sometimes that process starts with a single question, like this one, written by a U.S. veteran after five tours of duty in Iraq: "When the depravity of this world is laid out before you in its ruin, and you discover yourself mired in it, rather than above, what hope do you have?" (See Brian Castner, *The Long Walk: A Story of War and the Life That Follows*, p. 148)

War and captivity gave Francis a new critical lens through which to see the world in which he lived.  Increasingly, he saw



*Gillian T.W. Ahlgren*

the economic, political, and cultural forces of his day—as well as the religious structures that supported and upheld them—as dispiriting and even lethal. Slowly Francis turned what we might see as "disillusionment" into a clarion call toward a new way. The gift of these "lost years" of his life was his clarity about the brokenness of the world around him. His dissatisfaction with its message and assumptions proved to be a useful starting point for creative possibility. Francis teaches us the value of recognizing when something isn't working any more. Then humbly and collectively we can imagine something new.

**FOR REFLECTION:**

What has served, for you, as "a clarion call toward a new way"?

Has honesty about how something is not working ever given you a way to grow toward something new?

What do you find attractive about being part of "a community of mutual belonging"? What do you find challenging about it?

What have your experiences in your own community taught you about belonging, and what desires for connection do they stir in you?

# 3

# Stages of Metanoia:
# The God Who Is No Hobby

*No matter where you are from, waking up for the first time in Assisi is probably not entirely like waking up at home. First, there are the birds: sparrows, larks, and then, as you get up to throw open the shutters, swallows swirling around the churches, towers, and city walls. If, like me, you have gotten up for an early walk as the city itself is awakening, there is the delightful discovery of the daily rhythms of the townspeople: the sound of espresso grinding its way into small cups, café owners setting up their outdoor tables, merchants sweeping patios and entryways, and any number of courteous greetings as you step out to meet the day.*

*My mornings draw me either to the quiet of San Damiano or I get sidetracked, halfway, at the piazza Santa Chiara, where views of the gold-and-green-checked fields and valleys below Assisi invite me to pause and contemplate the olive groves, write in my journal, or listen to the nuns at the Proto-Monastery of St. Clare chant their way through matins. Each day a new beginning, each day an opportunity to meet God anew.*

But where will we find this God who wants to meet us? If Assisi teaches us how to encounter God, it does so at multiple levels, especially as we try to find God through the lives of

Francis and Clare. Their real stories are not quite as easy to discover or digest as we might think, and we will not meet them authentically if we are not open to a profound encounter with the living God who often surprises us in unexpected places.

We come to Assisi and are struck by its beauty—the medieval walls and buildings with their rose-colored stones, the deep greens of the fields, the sounds of sheep pasturing, the riots of flowers gracing the hillside. We feel the peace and joy that are part of the residual blessing of the city's famous saints. But as we piece together the winding narratives of Francis and Clare and open our eyes to the God they came to know and cherish, we come to appreciate the complex God of encounter, known in the many ways that we share life together and seek to make the world a place where all of us truly belong.

The first step in that journey is coming to grips with how many of us belong at the expense of even more who do not. It is a recognition that the "success" of some comes on the backs of many, and that this way of life is emphatically not the kind of human flourishing that God has in mind for us. There are many who have been abandoned, many who are routinely ignored, overlooked, even despised. As Pope Francis reminds us:

> We have created a "disposable" culture which is now spreading. It is no longer simply about exploitation and oppression, but something new. Exclusion ultimately has to do with what it means to be a part of the society in which we live; those excluded are no longer society's underside or its fringes or its disenfranchised—they are no longer even a part of it. (Pope Francis, *Joy of the Gospel*, par. 53)

Outcast. Thrown away. Left for dead. Did Francis's experiences as a prisoner-of-war give him a new sensitivity to the underside of daily life? Did his own experience of the fragility of life give him a deeper sensitivity to the legitimate needs of others? Did it give him new eyes with which to see those whom he had previously avoided?

The way of Francis and Clare is a profound awakening to the God who walks with us, drawing us to the margins so that, slowly and steadfastly, the margins themselves are erased, and a wider, more fruitful space is created. This awakening necessarily precedes the metanoia, or shift in perspective, attitude and action, that can then emerge. And this shift comes about because we go out of ourselves in order to encounter the reality of others. It is our isolation, our lack of encounter and interaction with those who can teach us about our world, and our lack of engagement with the complex social reality that keeps us small, individually and collectively. And it is arrogance to think that we can know ourselves or our world without engaging it in ways that allow us to grow in solidarity, empathy, and knowledge of others' experience. As Peter-Hans Kolvenbach said at the turn of the millennium:

> Solidarity is learned through contact rather than through concepts. When the heart is touched by direct experience, the mind may be challenged to change. Personal involvement with innocent suffering, with the injustice others suffer, is the catalyst for solidarity which then gives rise to intellectual inquiry and moral reflection. (Peter-Hans Kolvenbach, "The Service of Faith and the Promotion of Justice in American Jesuit Higher Education," Santa Clara, 2000)

As our minds and hearts slowly take in the reality of what our brothers and sisters unjustly suffer, we can learn, as Greg Boyle says in *Tattoos on the Heart*, "to stand in awe with what the poor carry rather than in judgment at how they carry it." More importantly, such encounters can get us to "rise up and walk" toward those whose burdens overwhelm them, catalyzing us not only into action but also into right relationship… into a solidarity that changes us and our world, as we learn to collaborate toward the common good rather than to act out of self-interest. As Greg Boyle describes this process:

> We stand there with those whose dignity has been denied. We locate ourselves with the poor and the powerless and the voiceless. At the edges, we join the easily despised and the readily left out. We stand with the demonized so that the demonizing will stop. We situate ourselves right next to the disposable so that the day will come when we stop throwing people away. The prophet Habakkuk writes, "The vision still has its time, presses on to fulfillment and it will not disappoint… and if it delays, wait for it." (Greg Boyle, *Tattoos on the Heart*, p. 191)

Francis and Clare located themselves at what Greg Boyle calls "the edges"; they experienced a true joy in living outside the city walls, close to the day laborers and outcast of the city. They felt and were affirmed by the fidelity and joy in embodying Christ in the spaces of greatest need as they attempted to make this world a home for everyone, especially those who typically had not been included in the kinship that communicates care, safety, dignity, and worth.

Most of us reading this book will have started the journey for meaning from a vantage point closer to that of Francis and Clare's when they were young, prior to their conversion. Like them, we may have some awareness of God—or at least of self and other—but these awarenesses may not have been informed by the God who does not want our piety so much as our radical solidarity and collaboration, especially as our minds and hearts

  *Gillian T.W. Ahlgren*

slowly take in the reality of what our sisters and brothers unjustly suffer. Conversion to this God is a slow awakening to the God who dwells in (and wants to teach us from) the spaces that seem unfit for God to inhabit.

Like Francis and Clare, we may be accustomed to look for God in churches and other sacred places, rather than in places of human disdain. In fact, we might find, to our chagrin, that our own habits, patterns and assumptions (as well as those of the cultures we are part of) work to keep us from actively knowing the incarnate God who draws us away from privilege and barriers and toward relationships that matter and change things. Francis and Clare show us a reliable way to be sensitized to that incarnate presence in the gritty world around us.

Being touched by God can be profoundly disconcerting, even as that touch quietly teaches us what it is to be real. It brings an intimate awareness of a tenderness within ourselves, a godly tenderness that we might not ordinarily understand that we possess. We may not know what to do about these awarenesses—how to act upon them or with whom to share them—especially at first. But this is the ultimate brilliance of "the way that God had with me," as Francis of Assisi tries to describe his life in his last word to us, his Testament. It is a way that is paradoxically both dramatic and initially confusing—not easily responded to, until experiences of tender encounter become a way of life. Some would call this process "incarnation"—a way of life constantly sensitized to the presence of God within the human community, a recognition and affirmation of the presence of God in our midst that helps us deliberately orient ourselves to becoming the kind of human community that God wants. Whatever we call this process matters much less than that we are deeply invested in a world in which margins are being erased because of where we choose to stand.

## Encounter as a Way of Life and a Transforming Process

Francis and Clare turned encounter into an arresting way of life, open to all. In their experience, there was no one whose life would not be deeply enriched by deeper dedication to the way of encounter. Engaging the other with the intention to listen, to learn, and to connect is a mutually transformative practice that slowly changes everything. Encounter teaches us to honor the fragility and sacredness of our own humanity, especially as we come to know our common humanity together. When done in the conscious presence of the love of God, encounter creates sacred space in the human community. Encounter moves us from observers of life to collaborators, with God, in the building up of the human community, the creation of a common home. Francis and Clare force us to ask ourselves what "conversion" really means, and to engage genuine conversion as a process: the quiet and precious gestation of something sacred, as we come to recognize and nurture God's tender presence, in us and in our world. Uncovering this presence is arduous; Teilhard de Chardin's helpful phrase, "the slow work of God," points to its subtlety and its sacrality. This presence is made all the more fragile by the precarity of so many, who live in circumstances of crushing poverty and horror: children sold into slavery, people routinely abused, and growing impunity for those who exploit them. The process of recognizing God's presence in our midst is as counter-cultural and even revolutionary as it is subtle, profound and thorough. It is a revolution of tenderness that re-writes what it means to be human. And it begins with the piercing recognition of the God asking us for help in the face of those who suffer injustice.


Francis and Clare's thorough commitment to the incarnate God was an ever-deepening awakening to the presence of God that each had already intuitively sensed, then actively began to seek, until finally they embraced deeply a revolutionary way of life. Both Francis and Clare could easily identify a moment of graced action that divided their lives into a "before" and "after"—a formative time in which the shape and meaning of their lives crystallized for them. But this was emphatically not a case of life "before God" and "after God." It was more precisely a summoning invitation from the incarnate God known at the margins of society, a "wake up call" to the presence of God in the drama of humankind that piercingly corrected many of the inaccuracies in the religiosity of their day. They had a growing consciousness of the presence of God in human communities free from presumption and pretense, where people sought a deeper integration of the simplicity and care that Jesus taught and modeled.

As he tells us unequivocally in his Testament, the most definitive description of "the way God had with me," Francis first learned the power of this incarnate God in one of the most frightening spaces of the medieval world: a leper colony. How did he get there? What led Francis to venture out into the space of the outcast?

We left Francis in the last chapter grappling with a growing awareness of his human vulnerability and with many questions about the values he had inherited from his family and his society. His return to Assisi, while a liberation from the hardships of confinement in the prison of Perugia, was not easy. He suffered, as we noted already, a "long illness" which required considerable time and attention to overcome. Medieval people lacked our contemporary psychological and medical understanding of post-combat trauma, but that lens helps us to imagine even more holistically the crisis of meaning he experienced after war and imprisonment. Perhaps an integral part of the "long illness" that then ate at him was the challenge of reflecting on the worth and value of his life up to this point and feeling that he had done nothing that was lasting, meaningful or significant. "Is this really all there is?"

Forced, first in the prison cell in Perugia and then on the sickbed in Assisi, to try to make peace with his heart, perhaps Francis intuitively sensed that following his discontent to its roots and seeking remedy and guidance from God from that space of vulnerability was not only possible but might be the only way to true happiness. The steps of conversion that unfold after Francis's imprisonment stem, ultimately, from this inner stirring, a divine restlessness that stimulates the desire to make one's home in two simultaneous places: the deep mystery of our hearts, nurturing a relationship with the God who is found there, and the world around us, that challenges us to find God in the ordinary, in the messiness, in the suffering, and in the joy that we find as we share life together. As we reconstruct the elements of this process, we can see that the crucified Christ, who reflects so absolutely the love of God-with-us, can speak to Francis so powerfully from the cross of San Damiano because, by then, Francis has himself already been pierced and wounded, body and soul, by the darkness of humanity. Thus, the prayer of Francis's heart before that cross was to seek true light and love despite and perhaps even within the reality of his humanity. What propelled him forward in a quest toward deeper integrity and purity of heart was the recognition and growing acceptance of his own brokenness, his incompletion, and the inner hunger of his heart for a wholeness he knew he could not find in isolation.

We can say that Francis's prison cell in Perugia provided the first real occasion for Francis to engage the space where his heart and the complexities of the world around him came together—ironically, a place of brokenness, in which he was surrounded by shattered dreams, unanswered questions, and his own undeveloped potential. Staying with that brokenness—being honest about it and coming to terms with it—allowed him slowly to explore his natural capacities of empathic understanding, solidarity with others, compassion, and cultivating loving relations, putting these gifts to use in the service of God and others. All of this would take time and patience to unfold. But Francis's time in Perugia left him unable to return to his life of aggressive and conspicuous consumption, which now held all of the appeal of shards of broken glass. Slowly, Francis found his former dreams far too small. Although he had, as yet, no other dreams to replace them, he was, at least, honest about the profound discontent he felt as daily life ceased to have any real meaning for him.

Francis's mother Pica appears to have had much greater patience with Francis's recovery process than his father Pietro, who expected Francis to return to the rigors of the family's luxury cloth business without further delay. Restless and unwilling to settle into his father's life, Francis conceived another plan. While in prison he had heard from a knight of Apulia about the bravery of Gautier de Brienne, a Frenchman in the service of the pope who had routed the German imperial troops. When another young man in Assisi, already of the noble class, spoke of his intention to join Gautier on crusade, Francis decided to go along and try to earn knighthood. Apulia was about two hundred miles southeast of Assisi. Francis got no farther than the town of Spoleto, when he decided to turn back and return home. What exactly happened on that journey is unclear, although it was definitive. Whether Francis had a dream in which God invited him to a different type of service than knighthood, as Thomas of Celano suggested, or he began somatically to remember what war had really been like, Francis quickly abandoned his plan. He returned to Assisi in the fall of 1205 only to face new suspicions from his father that he was a coward and a failure. The pressure to prove his worth intensified.

After his dream of military glory faded away, Francis's inner restlessness took on greater dimensions. His earliest biographer Thomas of Celano describes him at this time:

He prayed with all his heart that the eternal and true God guide his way and teach him to do His will. He endured great suffering in his soul, and he was not able to rest until he accomplished in action what he had conceived in his heart… He was burning inwardly with a divine fire, and he was unable to conceal outwardly the flame kindled in his soul… While his past and present transgressions no longer delighted him, he was not yet fully confident of refraining from future ones. (Thomas of Celano, *Life of Saint Francis* 1:3:6)

A simple prayer coming from his humble spirit epitomizes this searing time in his life:

Most High,
all-glorious God,
enlighten the darkness of my heart.
Give me true faith,
certain hope,
and perfect love,
sense and understanding, Lord,
that I may know and do
Your most holy will.

By the end of 1206 two major events provided Francis with a greater sense of direction; these events signal the convergence of a new orientation within him, one that would cause him to make a radical break with all that he had previously known. They are described in every biography of Francis, from the earliest to the most recent: Francis's encounter with the leper and his attraction to the ruined church of San Damiano whose crucifix became a focal point of Franciscan prayer. Not only do these events form the crux of Francis's inner experience of a living God, they also solidify and shape his external commitments for the rest of his life.

While they are distinct events, they are best understood in relationship to one another, as compelling communications from an incarnate God vividly demanding his attention. Solidarity with the suffering body of Christ especially as it is known at the margins of society gradually became, for Francis, the way into a whole new form of life.

In his own account of this period in his life, described in the *Testament* he wrote shortly before his death, Francis suggests that being drawn into the leper colony and the flood of feelings that overcame him once there was, for him, a singular expression of God's compassionate and tender love. Although we can and should speak of this experience as Francis's first knowledge of God's radical tenderness, it was neither purely sentimental nor was it an immediate denouement in the drama of his life. Francis's first experience of his sisters and brothers in the leper community did, however, suspend his malaise and despair by providing him a depth of connection that overcame him. In that connection, he felt a quickening of life flowing through him that now sought to extend itself into solidarity with people who had always horrified him. All of this showed Francis instantly and directly both who God was and who God called him to be.

Despised by society and condemned to a miserable life in colonies outside the city walls, lepers were absolutely dependent upon those few who dared to share the same bleak fate that they did. The radical ostracism of lepers in medieval society is hard to exaggerate. Francis's first real encounter with them in 1206 was hardly the first time he became aware of them. There were several leper colonies in the Spoleto valley, and Francis traveled through the valley often, whether on business or pleasure. But these colonies were places that Francis (and everyone, for that matter) always purposely avoided. Early sources record how "he used to hold his nose, not only when he saw lepers themselves nearby, but even their homes at a distance" (thus Julian of Speyer) and that "he used to say that the sight of lepers was so bitter to him that in the days of his vanity when he saw their houses even two miles away, he would cover his nose with his hands." (Thomas of Celano, *Life of Saint Francis*, 1:7:17.)

Francis's horror and disgust at the disease, in which flesh grew infected and putrefied until extremities rotted, was shared by all his contemporaries, who vigorously worked together to exclude lepers from any part of civil society. Even the church turned its back on them completely. Strict statutes were in place to keep lepers from entering the city walls or appealing in any way to Christian conscience: "No leper may dare to enter the city or walk around in it, and if any one of them shall be found, everyone may strike him with impunity."

Leprosy was a wretched and painful condition, but the suffering that lepers endured was more than simply physical. It was emotional, relational, and social. Lepers could neither work nor maintain contact with their families, and they had no identity beyond that of "leper." Their clothing, begging bowl, clapper, and warning bell set them apart from the world, and the leper colony was a place of isolation and despair. A ritual similar to a funeral rite greeted those condemned to the leper colony; to walk into one was a permanent sentence to a slow and painful death. No wonder Francis shuddered at the thought of the leper colony. It was not just disgust at the physical condition, it was also horror at the absolute helplessness and vulnerability of people there, many of whom could neither feed nor clothe themselves. No "self-respecting" person in Francis's society could or would associate with these untouchables.

Because Francis knew that it was beyond his ability to even want to reach out to them, it was easy for him to recognize the tenderness he felt for them as an act of God, a profound infusion of God's own love in his heart. As he describes his moment of conversion in the leper colony:



*Gillian T.W. Ahlgren*

The Lord gave me, Brother Francis, thus to begin doing penance in this way: for when I was in sin, it seemed too bitter for me to see lepers. But then God Godself led me among them and I showed loving kindness to them. And when I left them, what had seemed bitter to me was turned into sweetness of soul and body. (in *Francis: The Saint*, ed. Regis Armstrong, p. 124)

The experience was enough to change him forever, as he tells us: "And afterwards I delayed a little but then I left the world." (Francis, *Testament*)

The stunning experience of finding God in what was, for Francis, the most unexpected and unimaginable place—a place of horror and suffering—must have been profoundly disconcerting. And yet to have found love, connection, passion, and even joy in a place that he expected to feel disgust was also compelling.

As Francis began to accept vulnerability as an integral element of his own humanity, he found he had much to learn from those who lived with the pain of feeling rejected, ignored, and alone. For several years he had known that something profound was missing from his life: now the joy and fellowship he found with those left for dead gave him a new clue as to how to find meaning in his own life. Francis's initial experience at the leper colony had taught him what he already instinctively knew: "The joy of life comes from the ways in which we live together and the pain of life comes from the many ways we fail to do that well."

This insight, from Henri Nouwen's reflections at L'Arche, an intentional Christian community blending profoundly disabled adults with others, shows how life at l'Arche continually taught

Nouwen about God, about incarnation, and about being human. His reflections on the challenges faced by some in the community are particularly helpful to our understanding of what the experience of medieval lepers might have felt like:

> In my own community, with many severely handicapped men and women, the greatest source of suffering is not the handicap itself, but the accompanying feelings of being useless, worthless, unappreciated, and unloved. It is much easier to accept the inability to speak, walk, or feed oneself than it is to accept the inability to be of special value to another person. We human beings can suffer immense deprivations with great steadfastness, but when we sense that we no longer have anything to offer to anyone, we quickly lose our grip on life. Instinctively, we know that the joy of life comes from the ways in which we live together and that the pain of life comes from the many ways we fail to do that well. (Henri Nouwen, *Life of the Beloved*, pp. 89-90)

As part of our visit to the former leper colony outside of Assisi, we often read a passage that, for me, captures the essence of this wounding yet liberating moment for Francis. It is from Alan Jones' *Soul Making: The Way of Desert Spirituality*:

> Christianity is a shocking religion, although many of its adherents have managed to protect themselves from its terrible impact... It claims that the flesh matters. It insists that history (the particularity of time and place) matters. Above all it claims that, in the end, nothing else but love matters. Much of the discipline of the spiritual life is concerned with keeping the shock and promise of love alive. Without the occasional abrasive brush with the unexpected, human life soon becomes a mere matter of routine; and, before we know where we are, a casual indifference and even brutality takes over and we begin to die inside. The shock



*Gillian T.W. Ahlgren*

breaks open the deadly 'everydayness' that ensnares us and brings something awesome and terrifying to our reluctant attention; the believer's name for that 'something' is God. God ceases to be a subject for philosophical debate, still less the object of our part-time and casual allegiance. This God is no hobby. God is felt in places too deep for words… in pain, sorrow, and contradiction. This, in itself, comes as a shock, since we tend to make religion only of our better moments… One of the ways that the shock of Christ is kept alive is by means of 'compunction,' a kind of 'puncturing' of the heart. Compunction is the word for that which pierces us to the heart, cuts us to the quick, raises us from the 'dead.' Compunction administers the shock that is necessary for us to be who we really are—to wake up to our reality and our deepest truth… The will is liberated for action. (Alan Jones, *Soul Making: The Desert Way of Spirituality*, 84-85)

This description conveys, I think, some of what Francis felt upon leaving the leper colony for the first time. He had been "pierced" by a God felt in a place too deep for words. Whether it was the deep compassion he felt for the lepers' helplessness, his desire to make amends, through his trustworthy presence, for the ways they had been abandoned by his contemporaries, or both, Francis's experience of lepers as sisters and brothers before all else gave him a precious sense of the God who is no hobby. Their need for love, tenderness, and a community of care met his own, and they drew something out of him that Francis had not even known that he had. Looking back up the hill to Assisi, mustn't he have wondered where he really belonged?

*When I take groups down to the former leper colony down in the valley outside of Assisi, I often imagine the moment when Francis left that leper colony for the first time. His heart has been turned inside out; he knows something definitive has just happened to him. Something has now validated his discontent, this growing instinct driving him to question his life, its meaning, and all of the goals that have been imposed upon him by his family and his society. Now the hollowness of all that he himself has willingly and anxiously embraced is suddenly exposed for what it is. Forlornly, he looks back up the hillside to the city that has been home for him all of his life, that he has given his life and health to defend. Slowly he realizes that he is, in reality, just as homeless as the lepers who have shown him his own heart, and have given him access to the very heart of God. Although it is still a deep and shocking mystery to him, he senses that down here in the exposed plain of the valley, amidst those with nowhere else to go, he has finally found home. And a new and ultimate purpose for his life: to work with others to make the world a home for all.*

## From Encounter to Solidarity

Scholars who might disagree about how to interpret other elements of Francis's experience converge in noticing that his first encounter with God in the leper colony is key to understanding the rest of Francis's life. Many identify this moment as an essential experience of grace; it was the divine spark capable of igniting the revolution of tenderness to which Francis would dedicate himself. In the leper colony Francis discovered the living God. And in response he devoted himself to continually deepening relationship with the God who comes alive in loving encounter—the kind of ongoing encounter capable of changing our culture of indifference and exclusion.

Through encounter with God in those who were traditionally excluded and cast out of society Francis learned the fundamental characteristics of God: compassion, ever-abundant love and life-giving presence. Additionally, he saw that these fundamental characteristics of God came together in and through the incarnation—that is, the presence of God as experienced and mediated within humanity. The promise in scripture that, "where two or three are gathered in my name, I will be with you" was made real for him in each of those encounters. Encounter in its deepest sense is, then, sacramental, incarnational, very real, very human, and very sacred, all at once.

Francis had discovered, to his surprise, that God could be known, experienced, revered and nurtured in the human community, and it was the excluded and bereft lepers who had shown this to him. The coldness and superficiality of his own lifestyle was laid bare as he realized that, when it came to love, he had a great deal to learn from people he never expected could teach him anything. Together with his sisters and brothers in the leper community, Francis discovered a whole new way of experiencing the body of Christ known in *communio*, the shared union of God savored and enjoyed in community. Finding and sustaining that joy in community, as a living witness to the presence of God in the mystery of human relatedness, became a critical element of the new life to which Francis felt called. Increasingly, he doubted that such a life was possible within the city walls.

Still unsure about how to respond to these inner movements and where, exactly, to locate that response, Francis was drawn to a dilapidated church, also outside the city walls not far from the leper colonies in the valley below: the church of San Damiano. It is here that he was said to have understood the voice of God to say to him: "Francis, go and rebuild my home. Don't you see it's in ruins?" Rebuilding the church of San Damiano stone by stone became, for Francis, a concrete way to place himself in God's service, and the task of working thoughtfully with his hands gave him time to sort through his sense of God's invitation to him. Relieved to find something he could now actually do, Francis rode out to the neighboring town of Foligno to sell some of his family's cloth and a horse, returning to San Damiano with a monetary offering to the priest living there. Sources say that the priest, fearing reprisal from Francis's father, refused to accept the money, although he allowed Francis to stay there.

Francis's disappearance from the family home and business did indeed attract the ire of his father Pietro, who, by this point, found his son's behavior inexplicable. Pietro apparently believed that only discipline, punishment and confinement would bring Francis back to his senses. According to the legend tradition, Pietro locked Francis in a room in the house. After business drew Pietro away, Francis's mother Pica released him from confinement. Francis returned to San Damiano to continue to make good on his promise to God. Increasingly, Francis sensed that the work of creating a hospitable space, for God and for others, was his calling and the only thing truly worth doing. But this new way of life would require a definitive break from his father, from his friends and family, and from all of the social, cultural and religious assumptions of his day and age. The confrontation was not long in coming.

Returning from his business trip, despairing of Francis's sanity, and fearing for the financial stability of his entire life's work, Pietro formally requested a court hearing to have Francis punished. There was a civil protocol for this; in order to protect the family fortune, parents could have their offspring banished from the city on the grounds of parental disobedience. Pietro's case came before the civil judge in early 1207, and, when a messenger arrived at San Damiano to serve Francis with his summons, Francis claimed exemption from civil law because he was now working in the service of the church. The consuls referred Pietro to the bishop. The sources converge on this dramatic event: pleading his case before Bishop Guido outside the bishop's residence, Pietro demanded the return of the money from the sale of cloth and the horse in Foligno. In response, Francis not only gave it to him, but stripped himself of his fine clothing, standing naked before all and handing everything back to his father. In one fell blow, he had renounced his inheritance, his status in society, and his identity as the son of Pietro di Bernardone. The bishop, understanding Francis's dramatic gesture as a godly impulse toward a holier imitation of Christ, intervened by covering Francis's nakedness with his own ecclesiastical robe, signifying his endorsement of Francis's self-offering. In that moment, Francis left behind not only his family but all social structures, choosing instead to forge a new identity rooted solely in the most authentic imitation of Christ and the gospel way that he could imagine.

How are we today to understand this act? I see Francis's choice at three levels: personal, spiritual, and human. Leaving his family, his roots, and his life of privilege was obviously a deeply personal decision, even as it was driven by a desire to pursue a deeper relationship with God in line with the demands of the gospel. But it was also deeply human, and, as such, it entailed the whole of his personhood, in an attempt to reclaim his humanity and his integrity. It was Francis's *humanity* that was being compromised by the political, economic, social, and religious structures. And they compromised others as much as they compromised him.

It was commonly assumed that people would display contempt toward those who lived in the leper colony, begged for a living, or otherwise lived in the margins of society. In understanding the cost of such contempt for others to his humanity (not just his soul), Francis was making a compelling case for the need to free ourselves from anything that debases any and all of us. I think of this as a statement of personal integrity as well as a prophetic statement to the whole human community, almost like saying: "Our way of life so compromises my integrity that I must divest myself from it. I may not know exactly who I am being called to become, but I do know that I cannot become who I must without setting off upon an entirely different way." Francis's departure from his family, his social class, and the many ways that his life was being determined for him was an act of fidelity to the God who was inviting Francis to a very simple way: Act justly, love tenderly, and walk humbly with our God. (Micah 6:8)

It is neither too stark nor too simplistic to understand that Francis's encounters at the margins were revealing inconsistencies in his life and culture, and they now made certain demands of him. They asked him to choose toward a new and "wonderfully complicated" way of being connected to others. As Pope Francis writes:

> Sometimes we are tempted to be that kind of Christian who keeps the Lord's wounds at arm's length. Yet Jesus wants us to touch human misery, to touch the suffering flesh of others. He hopes that we will stop looking for those personal or communal niches which shelter us from the maelstrom of human misfortune and instead enter into the reality of other people's lives and know the power of tenderness. Whenever we do so, our lives become wonderfully complicated and we experience intensely what it is to be a people, to be part of a people. (Pope Francis, *Joy of the Gospel*, par 270)

Like Francis so many centuries ago, we are being called to the same kind of ever watchful scrutiny of the times, so that, with a similar clarity of vision, we can say no to an economy of exclusion and inequality, to the "dictatorship of an impersonal economy lacking a truly human purpose" and the tyranny of a consumption that "unilaterally and relentlessly imposes its own laws and rules." As Francis of Assisi saw so clearly, "an evil embedded in the structures of a society has a constant potential for disintegration and death. It is an evil crystallized in unjust social structures, which cannot be the basis of hope for a better future." Pope Francis, *Joy of the Gospel*, pars. 55-56, 59)

In turning his back upon dehumanizing political, economic,

social and religious structures, Francis freed himself to explore a new way of being human. Although he did not set out to start a new movement, I think that it quickly became clear to him that he would make little real progress on this way alone. Francis had been drawn into a new kind of personhood through the community of lepers down in the valley. Now, taking the cloak of a beggar, Francis began to live outside the city walls with lepers and outcasts, completing the reconstruction of San Damiano and beginning to receive people there to live together in poverty, simplicity, and service. As the fledgling community grew, its affiliates began to restore other churches in the area, including the church of Santa Maria degli Angeli on a small portion of land in the valley known as the Portiuncula. And at this moment Francis's life narrative and Clare's began to converge.

While Clare was not likely present at Francis's dramatic self-stripping in the courtyard outside the bishop's palace, she surely knew of it. The changes in his behavior and the escalating confrontation between Francis and his father had been fodder for public gossip, which would have reached her in one form or another. But Clare's understanding of Francis's growing estrangement with the socio-political world of Assisi would have differed from that of most of her friends and family. In fact, she was quite sensitive, from her own lived experience, to the same tensions with which Francis struggled. She saw, as he did, that the predominant social, economic, political and even religious norms of their day were not consistent with the simplicity of the gospel.

Clare was as cognizant as Francis was of the deep and inherent compromises to their humanity that success in their socio-political spheres and family circles entailed. She recognized that this diminution of humanity cut across lines of class and gender, impacting both the noble and merchant classes. Owning property meant defending property—and the cost of this was dear. As Joan Mueller cogently notes:

Clare and Francis had both grown up with and experienced firsthand the consequences of violence, riots, ambushes, and battles. Their families had grown rich off the backs of the poor. The youth of Assisi was losing heart with the constant struggle to have more and more. While the appetite of their fathers was insatiable, the sons and daughters of Assisi seemed to be sickened by the very thought of continuing the gluttonous struggle to acquire more… This social context makes Francis's and Clare's choice of poverty understandable. In an era when families fought families, and churchmen and monastics were entering into litigation to protect and expand wealth, Assisi's children saw that they had no future if they continued the behavior of their parents. If Francis had taken the way of his father, he probably would have died on a battlefield without singing for the world his *Canticle of Creation*. If Clare had not run away from the prison of her noble palazzo, she might have ended her days as a widow grieving over her husband and sons who died on some field for a senseless purpose. Instead, Francis, the merchant, and Clare, the noblewoman, made another choice. They called their choice "poverty." (Joan Mueller, *Clare of Assisi: The Letters to Agnes*, pp. xiv-xv)

And yet what others saw as poverty and renunciation Francis and Clare knew to be freedom and integrity. An early document, *The Anonymous of Perugia*, describes an exchange between Francis and the local bishop in which Francis expresses this sentiment clearly:

One day, when the blessed Francis had gone to that bishop, the bishop told him: "It seems to me that your life is very rough and hard, not having or possessing anything in this world." The saint of God answered: "Lord, if we had any possessions, we would need arms to protect them because



*Gillian T.W. Ahlgren*

they cause many disputes and lawsuits. And possessions usually impede the love of God and neighbor. Therefore we do not want to possess anything in this world." And this answer pleased the bishop. (see *Anonymous of Perugia* in Regis Armstrong, ed., *The Founder*, p. 41)

Francis and Clare's collaboration started early; Clare would have been only about fifteen years old. From the testimony of her family members and early friends gathered prior to her canonization, we know that Clare had made a habit of giving to the poor out of her portion of the household purse. Through the year 1208, as Francis continued his work of restoring churches outside the city walls, Clare showed her solidarity with him by sending money down to those working on the Portiuncula to sustain them. As she came of age, her financial support grew, extending into her dowry and even a portion of her sister's.

As Francis began to engage more actively in preaching, he returned to the piazza outside of the church of San Giorgio where he had been educated as a boy and also to the piazza San Rufino just outside Clare's house, where she would have heard his words. Francis's preaching and the simplicity of his life was already attracting others willing to give up their wealth and social position, just as Francis had. One of the earliest of these was a wealthy, educated nobleman named Bernardo di Quintavalle, whose dedication to poverty must have caused as much public scandal as Francis's had. Bernardo had degrees in both civil and canon law and he was much respected around the city. After consulting with Francis, he liquidated his extensive assets, including land on the hill and in the valley below Assisi, olive groves and vineyards. All the proceeds were given away to the poor. Joined by another doctor of law, Peter of Catania, and one of Clare's own cousins, Rufino, the group settled into the Portiuncula down in the valley. In the fall of 1209, Francis and his companions decided to leave Assisi on a lengthy preaching tour; according to Thomas of Celano, two of them went as far as Santiago de Compostela in northwestern Spain. Francis was living his dream of the gospel life, practicing as precise an imitation of Christ as he knew.

But leaving the confines and jurisdiction of the Spoleto valley required more ecclesiastical support than the bishop of Assisi could grant. As Francis's revolutionary way of life began to catch on, it attracted attention, notoriety, and the possibility of resistance on many fronts. In 1209 or 1210, Francis wrote out a simple, gospel-based way of life, and went with his brothers down to Rome to seek papal approval of this new way. The encounter of Francis with Pope Innocent III deserves some consideration, particularly because commentators often use the event to demonstrate either Francis's "uniqueness" (in other words, so the argument runs, he must have been recognizably different from his contemporaries in order to have so easily received papal approval) or a strong urge toward orthodoxy and obedience. Neither of these views captures either the encounter or its significance.

Francis was hardly unique in his desire to embrace the gospel life. Throughout the twelfth century, many groups, often founded by lay people, sought access to the gospels so that they could understand and align their lives with the teachings of Christ. When compared with the lifestyle of Jesus and his early companions, the wealth and privilege of church officials demonstrated all too clearly the need for major change. But genuine reform would need to extend into the entire church, requiring collaboration with Rome and with local bishops. Jurisdictional disputes over preaching had been cause for challenges to other lay groups equally as sincere and committed to their faith as Francis and his companions. A formal relationship with the church universal was necessary if Francis's gospel way of life was truly going to impact people outside of his corner of the world. Forging a positive working relationship with the papacy was a goal of reform groups whenever possible. Given the many levels of controversy over authority within early thirteenth-century church and society, it would have been irresponsible for Francis to have sent his companions out into foreign territory without some way of protecting them from situations that might lead to misunderstanding or accusations of heresy.

What is also important to understand is that many, many forms of religious life were created throughout the twelfth century, nearly all of them responding to the ethical and spiritual crisis triggered by the rise of urban economies. Many laypeople saw the urgent need for an authentic witness of poverty and accompaniment with the poor. Increasingly, this approach became a moral and spiritual imperative as Europe's feudal, agrarian economic system gave way to the complexities of a market-based economy, and urban centers ate through the poor and left them, literally, to die on the streets. The call to "go and sell all you have" in order to walk with Jesus Christ in poverty took on renewed meaning and urgency in the twelfth and thirteenth centuries, because the growing market-based economy challenged Christians to strip themselves of an identity forged by social status and economic standing and devote themselves more explicitly to simplicity and the social principles of the gospel.

What Francis wanted to re-capture and live was what the earliest companions of Christ had experienced: the presence of God coming alive in the human community. He wanted that to be the universal Christian way. Francis saw the living God in the discarded, and he wanted everyone else to see God there, too. He understood the forces that he and his contemporaries were up against. He saw how his own neighbors closed their eyes to the suffering poor, built walls to protect their consciences, and even discarded those who were unproductive. But in leper colonies and at the margins God was showing him how to remediate human exploitation through a tenderness that cherished those considered worthless. And the joy of seeing God come alive once again was not something he could keep to himself.

Francis saw all of this simply. He was interested in establishing a home for God in the human community—a place that Jesus would recognize because it welcomed the stranger, fed the hungry and clothed the naked. He wanted everyone to pursue a shared desire and a shared commitment to find Christ incarnate in our midst, without walls and without exclusion, and he did not think that any endeavor short of that was particularly Christian. In human terms, he wanted to be "someone who, through kindness, tenderness, and focused, intense love can return people back to themselves." (Greg Boyle, *Tattoos on the Heart*, p. 192). Francis's sense of church was one of constant extension, solidarity, accompaniment and communion. In fact, in many ways Francis's embodiment of poverty, simplicity and tender care was a way of teaching the church what it was to be a genuine community. For some, it was a reminder of gospel values forgotten after decades of civil and ecclesiastical conflict over wealth, territory, and power. For others, it was a new vision entirely. For all, however, there was a definitive stirring of the Spirit—a radical attentiveness to the demands of the gospel resulting in the kind of *metanoia* that Jesus had embodied. Innocent III saw, in Francis and his companions, a trustworthy witness of that model and gave his approval to their way of life.

As they walked back to Assisi, contemplating their new status within the church at large, Francis and his brothers asked themselves how they could best be a living example of the gospel. They stopped near the city of Orte for about two weeks to allow their new way of life to crystallize for them, committing themselves to the daily precariousness of the poor and homeless by begging each day for the food they needed to



*Gillian T.W. Ahlgren*

sustain themselves. When they continued on their way, they spoke with greater confidence about the gospel message and the characteristics of the kingdom of God they felt called to approximate, preaching with more boldness and clarity than ever. The personal charism and authenticity of Francis's witness, combined now with papal approval of his way of life, led to rapid and exponential expansion of Francis's experiment in community. The movement toward more authentic imitation of the gospel aroused both great hope and renewed commitment in Francis's contemporaries—women as well as men.

Clare, for one, was ready to become an active and equal partner with Francis in this gospel way of life. We have already noted her significant financial and moral support for the movement. But until this way of life had some kind of official status within the church, far beyond the support that the local bishop could offer, it would have been just about impossible for Clare to join forces more actively with him. I suspect, however, that Clare had already been mentally preparing to join the reform and was merely awaiting Francis's return from Rome with papal approval before cutting the final cord to her life within the city walls. Clare's childhood friend Bona of Guelfuccio testified that Clare had given her money to take down to "those who were working on Saint Mary of the Portiuncula so that they would sustain the flesh," thus confirming Clare's active collaboration with Francis in this new way of life as early as 1208 or 1209, since the brothers completed the church before they went to Rome for papal approval.

The testimony of the women who knew Clare best supports this emerging portrait of a woman of conviction, commitment, prudence, and courage, prepared to offer her spiritual giftedness to what she understood to be the most authentic version of the gospel life she could embrace. Bona, who had accompanied Clare as a chaperone during her early conversations with Francis, was aware that the two of them together had developed a plan that would allow Clare to enter Francis's way of life. Clare's natural sister, Beatrice, reports:

> After Saint Francis heard of the fame of her holiness, he went many times to preach to her, so that the virgin Clare acquiesced to his preaching, renounced the world and all earthly things, and went to serve God as soon as she was able. After that she sold her entire inheritance and part of that of the witness and gave it to the poor. (See "The Twelfth Witness in Acts of the Process of Canonization" in Armstrong, *Clare the Lady*, p. 183.)

The fact that Beatrice says that Clare went "as soon as she was able," underscores both the need for the institutional stability of Francis's way of life before women could leave their households to join him and the fact that Clare was already waiting without hesitation to join him fully in the growing movement.

Clare's departure from the world inside the city walls was no less dramatic than Francis's own. Late at night on Palm Sunday Clare escaped from her family's palace, hurried down the narrow city streets, and passed through the gates of the city walls for the last time in her life. It is not difficult at all to imagine young Clare's excitement, after months of planning and preparation. Slipping out under cover of night, she successfully made her way through the valley to the Portiuncula where Francis and several companions waited for her. Once Francis had tonsured and clothed her in a habit and veil, they departed for the Benedictine convent of San Paolo delle Abbadesse about four kilometers from Assisi.

Of all the options Clare might have had for safe haven, Francis and Clare had chosen this destination because a papal bull of Innocent III dated May 5, 1201 granted the community broad and specific rights of asylum to take in women in distress. The edict

                                          *Gillian T. W. Ahlgren*

forbade the use of violence against the women under the pain of excommunication. Clare had likely anticipated the active resistance of the men in her family to her decision to embrace poverty and the apostolic life, and had chosen a place where she could expect safety and insulation from any reprisals from her family.

It was all the more shocking, then, that the very next day Clare's male relatives pursued her and stormed into the monastery's chapel in order to bring her home by force if necessary. In an attempt to escape their wrath and protect herself, Clare grabbed the church's altar, claiming the right of the convent's sanctuary and special protections. Uncovering her head to show the men that they were too late, she revealed her shorn hair, the physical evidence that she had already vowed herself to God and made herself unmarriageable. Confounded, the men reluctantly made their empty-handed return to Assisi.

Clare had won the first battle and now, without the need for Benedictine asylum, she moved to the church of Sant'Angelo in Panzo, a small monastery of penitential women, which seemed more suited to the poverty she desired. Clare had thwarted her family's grandiose plans to marry her off and protect their wealth for future generations, and the men in the family smoldered. No one—not even Clare herself—anticipated the slow exodus, as her sisters and eventually her mother joined her.

Clare's sister Catherine appeared at the church of Sant' Angelo fifteen days after Clare had slipped away, confiding to her sister her own desire to join the new gospel way. This turn of events caught Francis and Clare by surprise and less prepared for the next confrontation with Clare's male relatives than they had originally been. The men, in turn, were even more violent at the realization that they had lost another of the family's most treasured assets. Because she had not yet been tonsured or made her vows, Catherine was far more vulnerable to the knights who appeared at the church of Sant'Angelo to bring Catherine home by force. They began to strike Catherine, ripping her clothes and crippling her with blows. Reconstructing this scene from the sources, Joan Mueller writes:

> When the knights of the family heard that Catherine escaped, they went to the humble and unfortified Monastery of Sant'Angelo, captured Catherine, and when she resisted their efforts to take her back home, beat her until she seemed lifeless. Perhaps too embarrassed to bring back into town a young woman ignobly beaten by men whose honor depended on providing her protection, they rode off, leaving Agnes for dead. (Mueller, *Clare of Assisi: The Letters*, pp. 12-13)

Clare nursed her back to life, and when Francis arrived to receive Catherine and tonsure her, he suggested that she take the name "Agnes" after the early Christian martyr because of the violence she had suffered.

I have recounted Clare's personal story at some length because this context helps us to understand that there was a deep strategy to the community that Francis and Clare were creating. Neither of them was a stranger to trauma and violence; their communities of solidarity and care were havens from outside forces, even as they were spaces of creative resistance and transformation. Further, their context is not all that different from our own. Clare's experience of violence in the home asks us to be aware of how deeply and intimately violence can permeate our personal lives, especially if we are women. We cannot afford to ignore the reality that the relationships that are supposed to provide support, comfort, solace, and joy are so often toxic and even lethal. Adrienne Rich once famously called the family home the most dangerous place in America for women, and the



*Gillian T.W. Ahlgren*

U.S. Department of Justice estimates the number of victims of domestic violence to be at least 1.1 million people annually. We ignore the epidemic of violence against women at our own peril and cannot speak of human well-being without ensuring that homes and families are safe for women and children.

As we begin to explore Francis and Clare's gospel way, it is helpful to remember that we need to ground this revolution of tenderness in the world in which we live: a world that is often hostile, toxic, and even lethal, to some of its most tender members. This way of tenderness requires an inner resolve, a steely strength, and a tenacity that might at first seem to contradict what we stereotypically think of as "tenderness." Over and over, as we contemplate the example of their lives, Francis and Clare will surprise us. They were **strategic:** they successfully predicted the violent response of Clare's male relatives and did everything they could to counter its impact; they were profoundly **courageous**, taking risks in order to ensure that their movement grew and thwarting resistance on many fronts; and they understood the need to **create a protective space** for the nurturance of the relationships that give life. They understood, in short, and committed themselves to a growing solidarity that had the capacity to change the predominant paradigm of violence in their day.

Francis and Clare's prophetic stance in rejecting all dehumanizing elements of life models what Pope Francis in The Joy of the Gospel has called "evangelical discernment." Francis and Clare give us a clear principle for daily life. They rejected whatever diminished or devalued the holiness of each human encounter, and therefore they model for us how to say "no" to the many forces in our world that "threaten the life and dignity of God's people." (See Pope Francis, *Joy of the Gospel*, par. 51) As the drama of their initial conversion gives way to the larger context of forming life-giving communities of care, hope and vision, they help us see how our deepening conversion to solidarity creates a space for God to come alive more fully in our own world. For Francis and Clare, radical poverty (saying "no" to all that dehumanizes us) is concurrently a way to make more space for the indwelling presence of God in our communities. Embracing our mutual belonging requires us to acknowledge a shared future and build it together.


As dramatic and important as Francis and Clare's initial acts of renunciation were, their choices were merely the first of a long series of assents to their deepening dedication to the gospel life and the love that God grows within us as we choose toward that way of life. For those of us who walk in the footsteps of Francis and Clare, our choice is not simply a "no" to some things and a "yes" to others. Our choice becomes a question of how we daily make use of all of our thoughtful, deliberative, and affective capacities. Choice becomes a growing capacity to discern the implications and consequences of our habits, decisions, and commitments; a growing capacity to weigh and assess what will best lead to the deepening of God's life within us and within our world; a daily commitment to prioritizing actions and approaches that protect and safeguard our inner simplicity, our reverence for creation, self and other.


In short, choice becomes a deliberate, intentional, and life-long decision to be faithful to the process of collaborating with the unfolding mystery of God in our lives. When we truly dedicate ourselves to God, we find, as Francis and Clare did, that we are dedicating ourselves to an evolving partnership that has no end and no limits, a partnership whose end we cannot entirely know or predict. For such a process to be set fully in motion requires a set of commitments, supports, and even freedoms from social expectations and cultural norms. The process that looks, from the outside, like renunciation and deprivation, is far more creative, empowering, liberating and joyous than we think.


                                    *Gillian T.W. Ahlgren*

When we trace these dramatic moments in our Spiritual Immersion Experience, we pause, at the end of this day to reflect on how radical but life-giving Francis and Clare's "yes" to God really was. Saying "no" to so much allowed them to experience a deeper fullness, of God and of life, than they could have known within the confines of the city walls or the lives that their culture and society required of them. Perhaps what should stand out for us was their early (and consistent) clarity that to embrace a life of joy, meaning and authenticity required them to literally opt out of the economic, social, political, and even religious dimensions of a world that encroached upon and threatened their very souls. In doing so, they said "no," directly and indirectly, to the people that were closest to them—family members and friends, some of whom could not help but take personally their rejection. But others saw the truth of their vision. The poverty that Francis and Clare chose was not punitive or renunciatory but a poverty that embraces the hardships that love sometimes requires of us. In fact, it was a poverty embraced in order to love more fully and completely, a poverty that allowed Francis and Clare to learn how to dwell in the graciousness of God.

Francis and Clare said "no" to their families with their myriad of expectations and gave up their socio-economic status in order to embrace a way of life. But perhaps we forget that this was a way of life that had to be created as they went. It wasn't as if they walked out of one world and right into another.

Francis describes the slow work of creating a path forward simply, even starkly, in his *Testament*, at the end of his life, when he writes: "No one showed me what I had to do." Only slowly and gradually did "the Most High reveal to me that I should live according to the pattern of the Holy Gospel." (Francis of Assisi, *Testament*, par. 14)

Francis and Clare had to discover, uncover, and create, together, an environment and a community that honored God at all times and in all places—in the poor and despised, in the meek and suffering.    It was in the small, the simple, the unnoticed, and the overlooked spaces that they were able to find and behold the God they sought: a God of gentleness and grace who constantly showed kindness, welcome, and tender care.

I think that each of them, in their own ways, came to the conclusion that it was far easier to find that God by letting go of everything— all expectations, all demands on time, all considerations, and, certainly, all concerns and anxieties over possessions and upkeep of property—and, instead, celebrating the miracle of there always being enough, between the kindness of friends and strangers and the generosity of God, to move us to be thankful rather than resentful.  If this is a new way of being human, it is a way both of gratitude and human resourcefulness—a movement to notice, honor and take delight in the human capacity to be generous, kind, and attentive to one another.

It is also important to note that by embracing this new way, Francis and Clare chose joy. We so often see their renunciation as a kind of noble sacrifice, but I am not at all sure that they experienced their choices in that way. Their embrace of spiritual joy through simplicity and the celebration of the presence of God in daily life is an often-overlooked but essential element of the Franciscan way.  One cannot visit Assisi and fail to experience their radiant joy which permeates the city even today. While it is easy to focus on their embrace of poverty, Francis and Clare knew that their wealthy contemporaries, enmeshed in the defense of their wealth and pecuniary, consumptive ways, were far more impoverished than they. Francis and Clare knew the poverty of anger, bitterness, greed, and revenge and chose, instead, lovingkindness, joy and the fullness of life that generosity invites. In fact, Francis "mandated" the practice of joy, cheer, and graciousness in his rule of 1221, writing:

> Wherever the brothers may be and in whatever place they meet, they should respect spiritually and attentively one another, and honor one another without complaining. Let them be careful not to appear outwardly as sad and gloomy hypocrites but show themselves joyful, cheerful and consistently gracious in the Lord. (See Francis, *The Earlier Rule*, 7:15 in Armstrong et al., *The Saint*, 69.)

In a world as confused about pleasure as ours is, it is probably also important not to assume too early that we know what true joy is. What so often passes for delight and pleasure can easily pull us from the purity of heart that fills us with vitality and helps us to see ourselves and the world around us in ways that are constantly fresh. The joy that I speak of here is a joy rooted in simplicity of spirit. Our hearts may know and sense it, but we might settle, out of habit, for something far less than the kind of joy we can discover in and with God, in and with one another. This is a joy like that of finding something that we thought was lost or that we never knew existed—a joy that scripture likens to that of finding a lost sheep, a lost coin or, more to the point, the joy of recovering a loved one, as in the case of the return of the prodigal son. It is a joy rooted in the realization of our deepest hopes and dreams. It is a joy that one cannot realize on one's own, for it is a joy that, by its intrinsic nature, seeks to be shared. It is a joy born of love, and, because it is rooted in a relational reality that endures, it is also a joy that is not predicated on particular outcomes or demands. The joy that Francis and Clare knew and, in turn, shared with others, was the joy of life-giving love.

Choosing joy is not always possible in a world of suffering, particularly when our suffering is enmeshed in cycles of violence.

Violence is traumatizing, and it is right that we not only seek "deliverance from evil" but also that we protect others from it. Both Francis and Clare personally experienced violence—Francis both in the battlefield and at the hands of his father; Clare at the hands of her own male relatives. Both were able to see clearly that such a response was inappropriate and even sinful. They neither condoned nor, more importantly, *acquiesced* to such behavior. Instead, they turned their backs, definitively, on the relationships that compromised their growing sense of purpose, dignity, and integrity as friends of God, choosing, instead, the joy of an entirely new way of life. They sought and created safe space for their relationship with God to grow, realizing that putting oneself in circumstances that support one's inner integrity and capacity to love wholeheartedly is a deeply important choice toward God. It is an integral part of the movement toward the deepening of God's life in us and in our world.

Thus we should notice attentively, as we try to apply their insights into our circumstances today, that Francis and Clare did not establish this new way of life in their own homes or on top of structures that were, in their experience, functionally unsound and incoherent when viewed in light of the values embodied by Christ. Cognizant of the toxicities of their culture, they chose not to adapt the gospel to its norms but rather to create new norms that called all people to see one another differently. They taught accountability, embracing the freedom of poverty and marginality as a foundation for the creation of a new way of being human.

Francis and Clare understood the corrosive effects of an unloving environment—all that might fall under today's categories of "dysfunction" and "abuse"—and they separated themselves from contact with all that might compromise their integrity, re-engaging the world from a space of inner stability and within a community that supported the fruition of their search for deeper relationship with God. Dwelling in the sacred space of relationship with God was critical so that they could engage the world lovingly. Perhaps part of their great wisdom is that, while they sensed that they were capable of great love, they did not expect themselves to love in the wholehearted way they desired without the support of a similarly-dedicated, intentionally formed community. From what we now know about trauma—especially that of deeply patterned abuse, such as repeated experiences of childhood abuse—there is much wisdom here in recognizing and honoring the fragility of the human spirit and embracing our genuine need for community support in order to thrive as loving persons. For some of us—many of us, if we consider the statistics—this will require extricating ourselves from situations and relationships that wound our spirits and threaten our well-being in order to seek and create the relationships that love us into greater life.

The Franciscan legacy is not naïve. For all of their aspirations to simplicity, Francis and Clare also recognized that they had to be "wise as serpents" even as they were "gentle as doves." (Matthew 10:16) Their choice toward God was practical and replete with understanding of the human condition. They recognized the toxicity of their world and they sought to create an alternative space in which the love of God could flourish. The way of gentleness they embraced—the dwelling place for God they prepared in their hearts and in the communities they grew—had no room for anger or bitterness, but that certainly did not mean that they excused, justified, or tolerated violence and indignity. Instead, they sought, uncompromisingly, to create a space where purity of heart could flourish, where a serenity rooted in the wisdom of the Spirit could grow. This was possible only in a space of deepest safety, learning anew the gift of love and the gift of life in relationship with the One who is supremely trustworthy. Francis and Clare model for us the often necessary separation from toxic environments that frees us first to create new communities of possibility and second to work with new strength and support to transform the world. This paradigm becomes a more viable strategy for meaningful change than working within a system that is unable or unwilling to be self-critical or to set aside its lethal ways. If the observation attributed to Albert Einstein is correct—"No problem can be solved by the same level of consciousness that created it"—we will need a collaborative imagination to create what we most deeply long for.

Solving our problems requires us to grow beyond the smallnesses of character and vision that plague us, uncovering together a solidarity that dignifies and creates possibilities that, individually, we are unable to create. If love is, in the end, "the only light which 'can always illuminate a world grown dim and give us the courage needed to keep living and working'" (Pope Francis, *Joy of the Gospel*, par. 272), we shall need to allow and enable love to give us the new human intelligence that our species currently requires. For love is not just a transforming power. It is the only viable strategy we have left.

**FOR REFLECTION:**

Describe an experience of encounter that changed you or helped you to see something new about yourself or the world around you.

Francis and Clare faced considerable resistance to their inner instincts, especially at the beginning of their spiritual journeys. When have you experienced resistance to your own sense of integrity or inner calling? How did you respond?

If it is true that Francis and Clare give up many things in order to follow God with integrity, what are they saying "yes" to? In other words, what are they "choosing toward"? Do you sense any attraction to the impulse to leave certain things behind in your own life? What might that make room for?

**4**

# The Revolution of Tenderness: Knowing and Sharing the Love that Gives Life

Francis and Clare's tenacity and commitment gave them the freedom to create a whole new way of life. From early on they knew that this "new way" was not new but was a complete immersion into the gospel life, to live as Jesus and his companions had. But there was still so much to learn about how to actually *live* such a life, how to sustain it in community, and how to nurture a dedicated and life-giving communal relationship with God that would provide inner light and direction for daily life. If we are to understand what was truly revolutionary about Francis and Clare's way of embodying the gospel life, we must identify the core spiritual values that, together, support a love that gives life and helps us continue to grow toward what is noble, right, pure, lovely, admirable and excellent. (Philippians 4:8) And we will have to learn and integrate into our being that kind of love, for it may be that some of us have never experienced it.

In fact, whoever we are, we are far more likely to have received very false, distorted, or even deceptive messages about what love is, what love gives us, and what love requires of us. We should continually recall the somewhat forlorn phrase from Francis's *Testament*: "No one told me what I should do." Not only is no one going to tell us what to do, fewer people than we might like are going to teach us what love truly is. Like Francis, we shall have to forge a direct relationship with God, through prayer and through deepening relationships with those who have been or are being treated as if they do not belong and do not matter. This was the way that Francis learned to know and share the love that gives life, and it provides the map for metanoia for us today.

Over and over, in both the Hebrew and Christian scriptures, love is defined for us by God—a God whose tender regard for humanity teaches us about what matters in life. The prophet Micah states clearly that all God requires of us is three things: to act justly, to love tenderly, and to walk humbly with our God. (Micah 6:8) And Jesus, citing the Deuteronomic tradition, tells us that our one responsibility is: "You shall love the Lord your God with all your heart, all your soul, and all your strength and love your neighbor as yourself." Covenantal relationship with God and right relationship with one another form the core of both the Jewish and Christian traditions, and they allow for a necessary inter-religious dialogue that can guide our planet. Through such a dialogue, principles of reverence, justice, and collaboration can move us toward the universal solidarity that we and our world need.

Dedicating ourselves, inside and outside our communities of faith, to shared encounters with the Living God can help us learn new ways of living together sustainably and as a single human family. To awaken an experience of God in ourselves and others, and to be reminded of who we are and for what we were made, it helps to use "the language of generous, relational and existential love that touches the heart, impacts life, and awakens hope and desires. Young people need to be approached with the grammar of love, not by being preached at. The language that young people understand is spoken by those who radiate life, by those who are there for them and with them. And those who, for all their limitations and weaknesses, try to live their faith with integrity." (Pope Francis, *Christ is Alive*, par. 211) The more that we are drawn into this love and come to know God, the more that we desire to be instruments of that love.

In the previous chapter, we explored how encounter with God at the margins of existence led Francis and Clare to transforming relationships developed in an ever-expanding community of mutual investment and concern. We described the conversion and dedication that such relationships require. Now we have to ask ourselves: when all was said and done, what was it that propelled Francis and Clare through the profound changes that we have seen them make? The human community on this planet today surely needs the same metanoia that they model.

In this chapter we will attempt to grasp the dynamic of life-giving love that was so riveting, undeniable, and transformative for both Francis and Clare. Without learning and integrating the reality of that kind of love into our own lives, we will not understand Francis or Clare, nor will we be able to answer the call to change and metanoia that God and life offer us today.

To some readers it may seem strange to devote an entire chapter of a book on the wisdom of Assisi to love, especially when love is obviously a critical part of being human and something that many of us long for. But of all the things that have changed between the time that I wrote *The Tenderness of God: Reclaiming Our Humanity*, drafted in 2014 and published in January 2017, our thinking about love, our approaches to love, our hopes and expectations around love, and perhaps even our faith in love have undergone dramatic changes that urgently need our remediation, if we are to survive in the 21st century. I use "life-giving" before love as a reminder that not all of what we have been offered as "love" has been life-enhancing. If love is to dignify and transform our experience of life, then we must learn, integrate, and insist upon critical and necessary qualities of genuine love, and our communities must be safe for us to do so.

## Love as Compassion, Tenderness and Generosity

We have already seen that a profound and unique experience of finding love and connection in the leper communities outside Assisi gave Francis the courage to turn away from cultural norms and self-centered instincts, with a new focus to create spaces of belonging and mutual support. Communities of care where life-giving love is shared are under deep threat in the 21st century, where relationships are more transactional than ever: workers are dismissed without rhyme or reason, people swipe in and out of sexual relationships, loyalty is measured in terms of subservience rather than genuine desire to improve the life of others.

If life-giving love is indeed measured by the quality and depth of our commitment to the flourishing of others, we will need to crash through the boundaries of entitlement and self-gratification in order to develop a true generosity of spirit—one that infuses even the duties and legitimate demands of love with a quality that keeps our relationships from becoming transactional. The key ingredient still missing—the one that allows us to move from "hardness of heart," a human disposition that seemed to most concern Jesus—is what I have described as a tenderness that allows empathy, connection, commitment, and joy.

Tenderness is a learned habit, an acquired sensitivity born of solidarity and keen interest in the lives, challenges, struggles, and joys of others. We do not become tender because we want to, just like we do not become fit because we want to. Desire is important, but dedication is even more critical. We dedicate ourselves to growth in tenderness, just as we might to greater fitness or flexibility.

While it is common to read about the Franciscan focus on poverty and preaching and even their imitation of Christ, these



*Gillian T.W. Ahlgren*

phrases fail to convey what was special, even revolutionary, about their way of life. Deeper and more direct than preaching with words, Francis and Clare communicated directly God's tender care and allowed people to see love in concrete, practical action: encouraging, supporting, sustaining, protecting, cherishing, admonishing. People acknowledged and joined the "Franciscan revolution" because Francis and Clare illuminated the truth of love's power. They made palpable the life-giving presence of God in the human community. As others saw the possibility of life-giving love, they, too, wanted to experience and contribute to its transformative impact on the world around them.

Francis and Clare refine for us the challenge of being human, even as they helpfully illuminate the work of the Christian person: our challenge is to embrace an evolving identity deeply informed by the ways that God reveals Godself to us, with and through the needs of others. We do this by rooting ourselves in the love that grounds and anchors us in a life worth living.

Francis and Clare's experience, practice and embodiment of a tender, gracious, life-giving love is what made their imitation of Christ authentic and illuminating to others. Life-giving love is a radical, committed, relational love that changes everything and helps us to see others as sisters and brothers. It is a love that so wants the well-being of others that it is willing to enter into their lives and experience the world from their perspective. As a way of life, this love asks us to live out our deepest ideals about goodness and right action in all of our interpersonal encounters. Life-giving love helps us move toward a culture of accountability, embodying the love that does justice, gives life, generates creativity, upholds dignity, and will not allow violence or abuse to trespass under the guise of love.

Ultimately, it was this love that drew Francis into the leper colony and gave him his first taste of God. Life-giving love empowered Francis to reach out to others in the leper colony, to receive and be received in their community, and to find his way back to God and to his own humanity. Similarly, life-giving love will empower us "to run the risk of face-to-face encounter with others, with their physical presence which challenges us, with their pain and their pleas, with their joy which infects us in our close and continuous interaction." (Pope Francis, *Joy of the Gospel*, par. 88)

## Scriptural Insights into Life-giving Love

Over and over, both in the Jewish and Christian traditions, a special word, "lovingkindness," describes God's way of being in relation with us—a way that chooses love, compassion, commiseration, gentleness, kindness and care rather than judgment, harshness, condemnation, or alienation. We see the reality of God's lovingkindness described and celebrated most commonly in the Psalms, with important uses in the prophetic tradition of the Old Testament and in key gospel stories in the New Testament. In the Psalms God's love is celebrated as "enduring," as in the repetition in Psalm 118 of the phrase "Give thanks to the Lord, who is good, whose love endures forever." This love "comforts" (Psalm 119:76); it is a "life-giving kindness" (Psalm 119:159) that "safeguards" and protects us (Psalm 144:2). In Isaiah we read of the "great tenderness" and "enduring love" which God promises to Zion (see esp. Isaiah 54:7-10). Thus lovingkindness represents a reality of care that sustains human life: empowering, nurturing, challenging, comforting, protecting and inspiring us.

This is why I suggest modifying the noun "love" with "life-giving." At this moment of human history, we too may need a way of differentiating *authentic* love (which promotes the well-

                              *Gillian T.W. Ahlgren*

being of the other) from things that are called "love" but are more superficial, toxic, or self-interested and therefore fall short of what we are capable of. Rather than thinking of love as a feeling or emotion, we should explore love as a way of being in which our individual concerns, orientations, and awarenesses are subjectively conditioned by our relationship with another or others. Emotions and actions—such as care, concern, outreach, solicitude, empowerment, advocacy—emerge from that orientation. Love enables us to respond to whatever is relationally appropriate for the well-being of the other. Life-giving love communicates direct and trustworthy presence to others and allows for human flourishing. It is an active love that is protective, corrective, supportive, affirming, challenging, and whatever else others need for their deepest well-being.

Life-giving love is visceral, spontaneously expressing commitment, concern, and active, constant involvement; this means that it can never be an abstract idea. Life-giving love is instead a concrete reality, continually taking shape and form in the context of our relationships with others and how we live them out. It is recognizable by its spontaneity, immediacy, constancy, and trustworthiness. Because this kind of love teaches and transforms us, life-giving love is also a love that never leaves us. It is also a love that surpasses our expectation—surprising and even humbling us with its generosity. What an incredibly critical corrective for us today, in light of what so often passes for "love."

*     *     *

In the New Testament, Jesus models God's life-giving love over and over by being present to people in their suffering and sorrow and, whenever possible, relieving their burdens by and with his healing presence. Further, Jesus teaches what life-giving love looks like in action, describing it as the motivation of the parent who, seeing a homecoming child from a distance, hurries to embrace him (Luke 15:20) or as the motivation of the good Samaritan, who came upon the injured man and was "moved with compassion at the sight." (Luke 10:33) When the gospels describe Jesus as being "moved with pity or compassion," they are pointing toward the wellspring of love that Jesus both felt and communicated to others, adding a richly expressive dimension to human relationship.

In his analysis of the biblical connotations of the word "compassion," Albert Nolan argues that "compassion" is "far too weak" a concept to express the loving impulse of Jesus toward others. English, he says, does not really have a word to describe this deep and visceral movement from "the intestines, bowels, entrails or heart—the inward parts from which strong emotions seem to arise… a movement or impulse that wells up from one's very entrails… an eminently human feeling." (Nolan, *Jesus before Christianity*, p. 35)  For Jesus this feeling of compassion often extended itself into acts of healing and the restoration of the inherent dignity of those at the margins of society, often in practices as simple and concrete as conversation and meal sharing.  As Nolan notes,

> It would be impossible to overestimate the impact these meals must have had upon the poor and the sinners.  By accepting them as friends and equals Jesus had taken away their shame, humiliation and guilt.  By showing them that they mattered to him as people he gave them a sense of dignity… The physical contact which he must have had with them when reclining at table… must have made them feel clean and acceptable. (Nolan, *Jesus before Christianity*, p. 48.)

Seen in this light, compassion goes beyond a movement to be of assistance to the other, because it "ineluctably entails a movement of participation in the experience of the other in order to be present and available in solidarity and communion. Compassion requires sensitivity to what is weak or wounded, as well as the vulnerability to be affected by the other. It also demands action to alleviate pain and suffering," since compassion is a relational disposition that comes from our inner depths—a courageous, generous "heartedness" that empowers us to make a difference in the lives of others. (See Michael Downey, "Compassion" in *Dictionary of Catholic Spirituality*, p. 192.) As Rita Nakashima Brock describes:

> The profoundest intellect lodges in our heart where thought is bound with integrity, insight, consciousness, and conscience… Heart is what binds us to others, safeguards our memory, integrates all dimensions of ourselves, and empowers us to act with courage. (Rita Nakashima Brock, *Journeys by Heart: A Christology of Erotic Power*, p. xiv.)

When Francis tells us that the way of life that "the Lord gave him" truly began when God drew him toward the lepers and he "showed compassion and lovingkindness to them," we should understand Francis to be saying several critical things. First, the novelty of his loving impulse toward lepers, for whom Francis had previously felt disgust and even contempt, was a singular and noteworthy act of grace within him. Because it empowered him to do something that he alone could not do, the impulse to life-giving love was indicative, to Francis, of *God's* motion, *God's* desire, *God's* purposefulness acting within him. The wellspring of love surging within him and seeking connection with others was easily differentiable from Francis acting of his own accord. In that sense, we might call it grace. But we need to understand that this grace was not the operation of a foreign God coming in as a mighty power. It was a "quickening," a vital movement, drawing Francis into his humanity and asking him to join the rest of the human community. It was God coming alive, in and all around him—in a vital and living form of what the Christian tradition calls "incarnation." Francis's intuitive sense of God's love drawing him toward others was how he identified and recognized God coming alive in him. Further, he experienced, in that growing aliveness, the desire to share a life of dignity and joy within a community of love. The intense poverty and need of the lepers drew a new solidarity and a deeper generosity of spirit out of him, even as they taught him about the living God.

Leprosy reduced human beings to a single common denominator: debilitating terminal disease. The hopelessness of their circumstances drew Francis to offer them what little he could: the reassurance and comfort of his personal presence. It wasn't as if Francis could cure them, nor even alleviate all that much of their physical pain. He could not even restore them to their homes and families. But his concern for their comfort and well-being, inside and out, could, in its own way, restore the dignity that their illness, dependence and marginalization may have diminished. It could also, to a small degree, make amends for the hardheartedness of others who were so willing to banish and ostracize them. And it was in that humble, basic, and simple space of repeated self-offering that Francis came to know God in the holiness of authentic and sincere human encounter. But there was far more *learning* happening in the leper colonies than perhaps we have appreciated. It was in the leper colonies that Francis learned the power of love and the real truth of the gospel.

As Francis saw and experienced the living God in the discarded, he began to understand that the God he saw coming alive and flourishing in communities of care was precisely the good news Jesus had embodied. Rather than seeing the gospel as a narrative of the past, he came to know that the quiet work of God in the human community is the good news, and living in communities of new life is the only real way we have of knowing the truth of resurrection.

                                        *Gillian T.W. Ahlgren*

Love, hope, and the joy of sharing life together were turning spaces of death into vibrant communities where everyone belonged and everyone mattered. Far from some kind of utopian ideal or pious charity, these communities of life-giving love were a prophetic witness to God's desire to come alive in our midst, to help us move from being merely human to being constantly humane and to work together to build a world that is home for all.

It would be hard to overstate just how revolutionary and motivating the heartfelt knowledge of God's love was for Francis. Although some accounts of Francis's life try to spiritualize this, turning the encounter with a leper into a one-time event, this is clearly not what happened. Francis's relational solidarity with lepers moved him to relocate so that he could stay with them and attend to their needs. The tenderness and intensity of each moment of connection fueled in Francis a fundamentally new understanding of himself, his humanity, and his relationship with God and others.

As I hope is already clear, it is important for us to remember that Francis's contact with lepers was not located in a single moment of his life—as if connecting the suffering of the leper with the suffering Christ was an elusive spark of revelation. Living in affectionate solidarity with the outcast quickly became the vital center of Francis's life. Much is made of how impactful the recognition of Christ in the leper was for Francis, and rightly so. But a careful reading of early Franciscan sources makes clear that Francis considered spending time in community with lepers to be an integral part of the formation process to become a "lesser brother," as the early Franciscans were called. Thomas of Celano, for example, writes that after Francis and the early brothers received papal approval, they spent their days working "with their hands, staying in the houses of lepers or in other suitable places, serving everyone humbly and devoutly." (Celano,

*Life of Saint Francis*, I:15:39 in Armstrong *The Saint*, 218) Another source, *The Mirror of Perfection*, indicates that "the brothers stayed in the leper hospitals," and "Francis used to call lepers 'Christian brothers.'" (See Armstrong, *The Prophet*, 303.) Eating with, being with, and living with the vulnerable gave him a deeper appreciation of the sacred dimensions of human interaction. The "miracle" of Francis's conversion effected by ongoing relationship with lepers is not so much the change in his feelings from revulsion to pity or compassion but the slower miracle of transformation in Francis as he allowed himself to feel deep gratitude to them for all they taught him about himself, about God, about being human, and about God incarnate.

A phrase that has come to mean a great deal to me is probably appropriate here: "the pedagogy of God." When a friend first used this phrase with me, in the context of his work with the poor in Peru who, he had already told me, were his most critical teachers, the phrase rang true and seemed pathfinding. ("I went to the University of Chicago," he said. "But the poor were my real teachers.") Embracing the pedagogy of God challenges us to allow God to be our primary teacher. And several questions proceed naturally from our response: How will we engage an intimate enough relationship with God to be taught at Christ's side, just as those closest to Jesus were? And what has the poverty of Christ, Christ's solidarity with the marginalized, and what the poor and disenfranchised have to teach us have to do with the way that God teaches? These, I would argue, were exactly the questions that drew Francis and Clare forward on the way of metanoia. They are, at heart, relational questions; they involve a commitment to a new form of identity, one predicated upon relationships that enhance and change our lives. This is the invitation we face, underneath the chaos and challenge of our world. How will we embrace and support our living together in ways that honor God and dignify one another? Can this life truly become holy through encounters that enrich us rather than transactions that degrade us?

                                    *Gillian T.W. Ahlgren*

Only if we are willing to grow, to be changed, to have our assumptions and presumptions challenged, especially as we heed the invitation to accompany the poorest and most marginalized, and courageously to denounce and change the systems that marginalize and degrade. This is a solidarity that changes lives, a "stay with me" love (cf. Mark 14:34, Matthew 26:38) that refuses to turn its back on the spaces of human darkness that many would rather ignore or deny: the trafficking of children, the degradation of women, and all forms of modern-day slavery. All of the places where "hardness of heart" turns truly lethal and ugly, where human pathologies have led to suffering, degradation and a sick intransigence that dishonors our dignity as a human community and as a species.

A genuine turn toward a transforming solidarity at the margins requires a new, relational identity (as opposed to a more autonomous one, predicated on our assumptions, our personal goals, and the priorities and values we inherit from our cultures). For many of us, this invitation is likely to be at least as disconcerting as Francis's and Clare's insistence on material poverty. But if it is true that we need others to pull us out of the "smallness" of ourselves, then this relational identity is the cornerstone of a fertile creativity that grows as we join forces with others and allow the wellspring of the Spirit to release grace into the world through our connectedness. This is a solidarity that gives life to all—not just the marginalized, but us, too! What is ironic is that we continue to see Francis and Clare's journey in terms of renunciation—what they gave up— rather than in terms of what they gained: a genuine richness in the quality of their lives, as love and kinship deepened, and they showed the world that "there is no 'them' and 'us,' just 'us.'" (See Greg Boyle, *Tattoos on the Heart*, p. 190)

The love that Francis learned through his pivotal relationship with sisters and brothers in the leper community transformed him by encouraging his ever-deepening participation in the mystery of Christ's incarnation. This love was, of course, to be spread into the world, and here it is important to reiterate that this love is multi-faceted. Cultivating a genuine and human relationship with the marginalized involved growth in solidarity, empathy, compassion, humility, human vulnerability, and a sharper social and theological critique of the injustice and inhumaneness of marginalization itself. It is no wonder, then, that solidarity with sisters and brothers who were sick, impoverished, marginalized or otherwise suffering was an integral part of the Franciscan way of life: not only was it a sharing in the care and concern that Christ manifested with his contemporaries, it was also considered a fundamental foundation and orienting principle to our own humanity.

Both men and women engaged in this way of life. Clare made provisions for sisters to serve outside the convent; her rule for the Poor Ladies suggests that Clare was not oriented to monastic enclosure as a value in and of itself, but as a contemplative space supporting solidarity and lovingkindness. While her *Form of Life* does not specify the kind of work that "ministering sisters" engaged outside the convent, their presence in the community was meant to "constantly edify" others with virtue. Clare's *Form of Life* requires all Poor Ladies to live in absolute solidarity with the sick, impoverished and marginalized; this is their way of living out their commitment to Christ's own poverty and solidarity.

For women as well as for men of the early Franciscan movement, attending to the suffering bodies of their contemporaries proved to be an extremely important way of attending to the suffering body of Christ in the world and witnessing to the ongoing incarnation of God in humanity. The way of Francis and Clare shows us that there is no genuine imitation of Christ that falls short of such practical expressions of solidarity and love—a solidarity that changes us and changes our world. They help us to see that our devotion to Christ without clearly living into this transforming solidarity can easily become an insult to the suffering Christ in our sisters and brothers. They keep us from falling into blindness and having to ask, "Lord, when did we see You hungry, thirsty, in captivity, or in need of shelter?" (See Matthew 25:31-46) or from the agony of the rich man in Luke 16:19-31, who clearly knows who Lazarus, the beggar at his gate, is, but whose lack of regard for Lazarus costs the rich man dearly.

In conclusion we note that the way of Francis and Clare was a way of life-giving love that prioritizes a relational experience of personhood over an egocentric one, with an intentional desire to affirm, support and enhance the presence of God in our midst. Francis and Clare exemplified the power of God's own tenderness by translating what they had learned about God's love into a way of being in human community. The earliest communities, at San Damiano and the Portiuncula, were living schools, training people in the daily practice of loving solidarity, as this was modeled by Christ. The assumption in those communities was that all would be continually growing in the tenderness and life-giving love that protects, sustains, and supports the presence of God in the human community. What would that look like in today's world?

**Communities of Solidarity and Resistance**

Three elements characterize the communities that Francis, Clare and others were forming: (1) active care for one another; (2) solidarity, equality and invested kinship; and (3) prophetic resistance to injustice and sin. In this section we will explore Francis and Clare's vision of community as one that enhances life for all. In other words, rather than seeing their way as illustrative of a proper Christian life (which it is), I would like to suggest that their vision of community is deeply relevant to the entire human community, not just to Catholics and Christians. From its inception through its historical development over the centuries, Francis's and Clare's experience of the mystery and possibility inherent in being human had universal implications for humanity—implications that immediately challenged many of their own cultural norms and provided standards for humane and ethical conduct around the world. The intercultural and interreligious implications of their vision of community continue to emerge as people continue to gather in the spirit of Assisi and extend their way into a hurting world.

Francis and Clare embodied the gospel's invitation to engage our human interrelatedness, our responsibility to one another, and the holiness that being human involves. This is, first and foremost, a human journey, one of universal solidarity, in which the "slow and arduous effort" of becoming a people requires "integration and a willingness to achieve this through the growth of a peaceful and multifaceted culture of encounter." (For more on this, see Pope Francis, Joy of the Gospel, par. 220 and Pope Francis, *On Care for Our Common Home*, par. 14.)

Human community does not happen haphazardly. It requires intentionality beginning with our most intimate companions: those with whom we have actively *chosen* to be in community. For Francis and Clare, the new gospel way of life required them to form an intentional community that differed sharply from their families of origins. Their movement was a living experiment in community life, explored by others who felt as strongly called toward the demands of the gospel as Francis and Clare did, and it was informed by sharing life with those at the margins of society. A keen solidarity was forged through the shared vulnerability of all members of the community. As we consider how we today might integrate elements of Francis and Clare's vision of community we need to remember the importance of intentionality



*Gillian T.W. Ahlgren*

in community formation. A caring community of solidarity and resistance forms because people (1) want it to form, (2) are ready and able to engage the inner changes that forming such a community will require, and (3) can self-monitor and call all one another to greater integrity, maturity, and accountability. Such a community is one in which growth—individual, interpersonal and social—is a primary, core value.

The element of choice in our configuration of intimate community is important; we speak of this as an "intentional community," which, while it may take many forms, will always have a significant commitment, on the part of each member, to grow and to choose toward "what better leads to God's deepening life" in us and in our connectedness. As Parker Palmer explains:

> The core of the Christian tradition is a way of inward seeking that leads to outward acts of integrity and service, acts of love. Christians are most in the Spirit when they stand at the crossing point of the inward and the outward life. And at that intersection, community is found. Community is a place where the connections felt in our hearts make themselves known in the bonds between people and where the tuggings and pullings of those bonds keep opening up our hearts. (See Parker Palmer, *The Promise of Paradox: A Celebration of Contradictions in the Christian Life*, p. 90.)

Palmer urges us to consider community as a process as much as a place, writing:

> Community is another one of those things (like personal well-being) that eludes us if we aim directly at it. Instead, community comes as a by-product of commitment and

struggle. It comes when we step forward to right some wrong, to heal some hurt, to give some service. Then we discover each other as allies in resisting the diminishments of life. It is not accidental that the most impressive sense of community is found among people in the midst of such joyful travail, among those who have said no to tyranny with the yes of their lives. (Palmer, *The Promise of Paradox*, pp. 80-81.)

Relationships that explore and embody life-giving love are continually renewing interpersonal commitments at emotional, physical, and spiritual levels. They are therefore able to extend a similar loving graciousness in relationship to others. The way of life-giving love provides a context for discovering and nurturing human goodness and giftedness in one another as we express a willingness to participate in mutual support and transformation, expand the quality of one another's lives, and deepen our connections to one another through sensitive openness to what the other is experiencing. (For more development of this topic, see Rita Nakashima Brock, *Journeys by Heart*, pp. 47-8.)

Because there are both risks and responsibilities in such a community, there are also built-in assumptions about personal maturity, commitment to ongoing personal growth, honesty, integrity and sensitivity to the growth process in others. Not everyone is ready, willing and able to commit to the principles and ground rules that are necessary for the healthy functioning of such a community. But these are the communities that cause dreams to emerge, awaken a prophetic spirit, and create new possibilities for life on our planet today.

The community that Francis and Clare strove to build was not accidental but rooted in the intentional practice of life-giving love, as we defined it above. Such a community, in which interpersonal communion deepens over time, takes deep commitment to the

					*Gillian T.W. Ahlgren*

human potential that we glimpse in ourselves and others. The grace-imparting love of God is the foundation of such a community; it is not merely a human work. And yet God alone does not "make" such a community happen. Active, adult collaboration is necessary. We draw from the generous wellspring of God, in our depths and in our midst, taking both inspiration and vitality from the source of life that God's love is. Those who have not experienced this form of interpersonal relationship or communion may believe that it is ethereal, even impossible—another reason for us to move beyond an overly sentimental or emotional definition of love. There are critical elements to relationships rooted in true communion, known by and through their power to awaken us to a deeper sense of purpose, to instill wisdom in discernment (i.e., the capacity to make wise and sensitive choices, both individually and collectively), to encourage sensitivity to the promptings of the Spirit of God, to grow in courage as prophetic witnesses to a more just way of being, to inspire and provide the vision for individual and collective transformation necessary within structures of suffering and injustice, and to console and galvanize the human community at large as we take heart and draw strength from one another. To see the potential embedded in our own humanity unleashed, growing and flourishing in ourselves and others, is intrinsically joyful, mysterious, and inspiring.

Because it is both intentional and mysterious, it would be unreasonable and unwise to "expect" or "demand" that such a grace-filled process be an intrinsic part of every relationship or community. Experience shows us that only some relationships can nurture the flourishing of our deepest personhood. When we consider the early lives of Francis and Clare and the violence that each of them experienced within their own familial contexts, we should be aware that not everyone experiences and learns, from their families of origin, the friendship, or their intimate relationships, what life-giving love is. (For a profound and relevant discussion of this, see Brock, *Journeys by Heart*, pp. 1-24, esp. p. 16.)

Whatever our family history and background, we will surely have to continue to grow in love, creating the best community context to support how we embody the love that God invites us to experience. For Francis and Clare, saying "yes" to the love of God required a whole new context of relatedness and familiarity; it demanded a certain "no" to their families of origin with all of their expectations, as well as to many if not most of the social and cultural norms of their day. The community they created was the foundation of the gospel life they sought to share. Thomas of Celano captures this process of radiating love into the world beautifully when he describes Clare's way of prayer: "She opened more generously the depths of her mind to the torrents of grace that bathe a world of turbulent change." (See Thomas of Celano, *Life of Saint Clare* 19:2.). Living out the daily practice of tender care toward one another makes it possible for us to extend this practice out into the world at large.

For Francis and Clare, cultivating an intense and fervent love for all that is good, in the world and in others, is not a "soft" love that tolerated anything, but rather one that could love the suffering and disenfranchised at the same time that it admonished and called to accountability those who chose lesser, unloving ways of being human. It is instructive and somewhat lost in our traditional re-tellings of the Franciscan story that both Francis and Clare understood their way of life as primarily a way of penance—a way that they themselves followed and that they preached to others, by word and example. The earliest Franciscans were called "brothers of penance," and, in his Testament, Francis specifically refers to the origins of his way of life in the leper community as the way God gave him to do penance. Doing penance is a direct response to sin; without personal and social sin, penance would be unnecessary. Francis and Clare intended their way of life to lovingly invite people away from the patterns of sinful behavior that trapped them and oppressed others.



*Gillian T.W. Ahlgren*

How should we understand this way of penance? It is a way of constant conversion and change. It is a way of continual personal and social improvement, turning away from what diminishes our goodness and doing all that needs to be done to uphold, protect, defend, and support human dignity. Love, rooted in true solidarity with another, demands justice. When one takes the lived reality of another seriously, appreciating the challenges that the other experiences and wanting them to know the encouraging love of God, a keen sense of the other's dignity and worth emerges. Francis, Clare, and their early companions were sensitive to the injustices of their world and preached a prophetic form of conversion to the gospel demands of justice. Encouraging and facilitating a conversion to justice is an intrinsic part of the love that they embodied.

But the common kinship of all creatures is the key insight to understanding the way of Francis and Clare. We belong *with* one another, and we belong to one another. We share a common home, and we need one another, in a complex web of creation that is increasingly fragile. The web of our interconnectedness is as important to maintain as the individual cords of connection. As Michael Cusato writes, because we are brothers and sisters to one another, anything that breaks the bonds of our relatedness— through the destructive or abusive use of power or by placing oneself over and against others for one's own advantage—is what, for Francis, constitutes sin. To do penance, then, is "to distance oneself from all those actions and attitudes that threaten to rupture the bonds of the human family." (See Michael F. Cusato, "The Mystical Experience behind the Stigmatization Narrative of 1 Celano" in *The Stigmata of Francis of Assisi: New Studies, New Perspectives*, p. 70.) Francis and Clare's way of life is a prophetic denunciation of all that cripples and destroys human solidarity, friendship and collaboration. It is an embodied translation of the gospel into the kinds of loving action that make all the principles of the reign of God come alive.

That Jesus was rarely found in the temple but always available to those in need could not have escaped Francis's awareness, especially once he had been touched so deeply by the aliveness of God in the community inhabited by his sisters and brothers in the leper colony.  As the order grew and some in his own religious community refused to enter the leper colony (and therefore denied the Christ who was so palpably real to Francis there) makes Francis's *Testament* at the end of his life all the more poignant.  His statement to his brothers of "the way that the Lord gave me" can now be read as an urgent plea that they, too, experience metanoia and learn life-giving love from Christ in the leper colony: "Go there," the subtext might read, "and engage your relationship with those who suffer marginalization and the contempt of the world.  You will find God there, and be drawn into the mystery of God-become-human, God experience-able somehow in the midst of our own human community."

Because this subtext of Saint Francis's *Testament* may not have been clear to us across the centuries, Pope Francis underscored it for the 21st century.  In his message for the first World Day of the Poor (November 19, 2017), Pope Francis recalled the life of St. Francis as the Christian tradition's most outstanding example of conversion and solidarity with the poor.  "Let us, then, take as our example Saint Francis and his witness of authentic poverty," he said.

> If we want to help change history and promote real development, we need to hear the cry of the poor and commit ourselves to ending their marginalization…. Our prayer and our journey of discipleship and conversion find the confirmation of their evangelic authenticity in precisely such love and sharing.  This way of life gives rise to joy and peace of soul, because we touch with our own hands the *flesh of Christ*.  (See Pope Francis, "Let us love, not with words, but with deeds," pars. 3-4)

When Francis calls people to solidarity with their sisters and brothers in the leper colony in his *Testament*'s restatement of God's way with him, he is calling us to embody the principles and practices of the reign of God and suggesting that when we turn our backs on God in the leper or in any disenfranchised person, we betray God. The integrity of our witness to the gospel is always eroded by our aversion to the God made known in and through the marginalized. The turn toward this God was the way of metanoia that Jesus continually embodied. And, for Francis, this way was opened up by the sisters and brothers in the leper colony who first helped him come to know God, reclaim his humanity, and live into the mystery of God enfleshed.

In addition to being an admonition of sorts, Francis's *Testament* reflects his desire to share God with others, a desire that only grew over the course of his life as an extension of his embrace of genuine poverty. As his self-stripping increased, the only and truest "thing" he had left to share with anyone else was his experience of God and his desire to embody the generous love of God that he had experienced. Blind, lame, and increasingly able to do little more than sing the praises of God, Francis ends his life with a poignant invitation to all of us to participate and share in the unitive life, the mystery of God-with-us. Francis and Clare show us that drawing nearer to others and seeking their welfare is what opens our hearts to God's greatest and most beautiful gifts.

Because God had communicated to Francis, through the powerless, a new vision of community, he became keenly sensitive to the abuse of power as the root cause of sin. Renunciation and denunciation of power that is wielded over others rather than used to ensure the well-being of all is a critical element in his vision. The gospel that Francis and Clare and their earliest companions were preaching was a radical message of love that hoped and strove and worked for the betterment and deepest well-being of others, upholding the dignity of all God's creation. They show us a way of life-giving love that is unafraid to speak truth to power and to advocate for and embody the at-times radical changes that discrimination, injustice and sin require. In an unjust world, this kind of solidarity and advocacy is the logical corollary of the realization that we are one human family, living on a common home, and therefore we are all brother and sister to one another and to all creation.

*    *    *

The immediate problem in identifying love as being the heart of the new gospel life that Francis and Clare created is that we have no real context—cultural, religious, emotional or even theological—for understanding and appreciating the depths of this love or its demands upon us to ensure and uphold human dignity in the face of forces that daily assault it. Concurrently and as a direct corollary, we have yet to explore the capacity of tenderness to empower us into a new way of being that supports our putting gospel principles into action. Indeed, in some ways our own current impoverishment, as individuals, communities, and even as a species, is rooted in our inability to be capacitated and revitalized physically, emotionally, intellectually and spiritually through the dynamic power of love. Our understandings and experiences of power are so deeply entrenched in demonstrating power by force or coercion that we have less and less access to the realms of possibility that collaboration and creativity open up for us. And given the complexity of the problems that we face, it could well be that our very survival depends upon a fundamental shift in how we approach both love and power.

I echo Francis and Clare by challenging us, as I believe Christ did, to take the power of love seriously, placing all of our other resources as human persons—intellect, creativity, insight,



*Gillian T.W. Ahlgren*

wisdom, passion, wit, humor—in the service of the only vessel strong enough to integrate, temper, and direct our giftedness in ways that have the possibility of enhancing our well-being. In this sense, I am also attempting to be as faithful to and authentically representative of the Franciscan and the Christian tradition as I know how to be. If the fundamental insight of Christianity is that God is love, then there must be a power to that love that we have yet, as humans, to fully appreciate or enact in our own lives. If love sentimentalizes life rather than energizing, revivifying, and empowering us, making us wiser and better people, then we have missed the gospel message. Francis and Clare's simple and wholehearted desire to make life-giving love accessible to others, can continue to teach it to us today. Love gives us a perspective on humanity that we can gain in no other way except through our openness to the power of love. As we collaborate with God and with others more actively in love, a radical new way of being human is forged. Love is a power that can dissolve, undo, and reconfigure all other forms of power. We might prefer to deny that, rather than to engage the experiment in love that Francis and Clare model, because it changes just about every intellectual, social, political, even theological assumption that we have.

When Francis strips himself before the bishop and gives his father back his clothing, it is easy to see that as a renunciation of his wealth, his inheritance, his patrimony. More importantly, though, this divestment was a radical renunciation of power and autonomous identity. By walking forever away from his social status and access to wealth, Francis was not only "nakedly following the naked Christ," he was asking God for a new identity, an identity that was not rooted in power over others. He sought, in God, a personal and social identity rooted in the richness of his relationship with God and others, experienced qualitatively in terms of the intensity of connectedness and the transformative impact of communion.

As Francis had already instinctively realized, the path toward this new identity was best learned through the love he had experienced among lepers and the outcast. That love had already taught Francis more about power than his experiences of war, wealth, popularity and social acceptance, all of which had come at a tremendous cost to his humanity. Whereas his experience of privilege and social class had diminished his humanity, what Francis found in the leper colony was an *enhancement* of his humanity—a new richness that he experienced in and through his humanity because he found a connection to others and to his deepest personhood. Wisdom and insight into the incarnate reality of God and the communion that God's love makes possible within the human community were central to that new identity as a human person. The core texts that both left behind—Francis's *Testament* and Clare's letters to Agnes (which we will explore in the next chapter)—should be seen as documents that reflect their role as mentors offering counsel, solidarity, encouragement and inspiration in a new way of life. They are an invitation into a fuller experience of the mystery of God in the human community.

The way of life-giving love changes how power manifests and expresses itself in human relations. In addition to teaching gentleness, compassion and tenderness, this way functionally invalidates the use of power to dominate, abuse or injure another's dignity, even as it allows for the creative ways that life-giving love protects, defends and advocates for human dignity and right relations. The way of life-giving love recognizes that God chooses relationality over self-sufficiency, God wants to empower us with the gift of life and asks only that we act justly, love tenderly and walk together in the relational reality that comes alive in communion.

In theory, of course, Francis and Clare wanted to live in communities in which it was not necessary to impose discipline



*Gillian T.W. Ahlgren*

but rather where each member of the community freely embraced the values of the community and therefore needed mentoring, accompaniment, support, and counsel rather than much active coercion, remonstrance, or discipline. In so far as they had to legislate, they tried to do so clearly and simply, as in the following examples:

> Let them love one another, as the Lord says: *This is my commandment: love one another as I have loved you.* Let them express the love they have for one another by their deeds, as the Apostle says: *Let us not love in word or speech, but in deed and truth.* (Francis of Assisi, **Earlier Rule** 8 in Armstrong, *The Saint*, p. 72)

> Likewise, let all the brothers not have power or control in this instance, especially among themselves; for, as the Lord says in the Gospel: *The rulers of the Gentiles lord it over them and the great ones make their authority over them felt; it shall not be so among the brothers. Let whoever wishes to be the greater among them be their minister and servant. Let whoever is the greater among them become the least.* (Francis of Assisi, Earlier Rule 6 in Armstrong, *The Saint*, p. 67)

> And let no one be called "prior," but let everyone in general be called "lesser brother." And let one wash the feet of the other. (Armstrong, *The Saint*, 68.)

At a practical level, Francis appeared to want to use power over no one. Understanding communion as the root of all relationality and sensitized to the tenderness of true love, exerting power over another likely felt to Francis like a violation of the inherent holiness rooted in the relationship. By the end of his life, if we are to believe Thomas of Celano's *First Life*, Francis wanted nothing more than to "return to serving lepers and to be held in contempt, just as he used to be." It pained him to see that the popularity of his movement had actually neutered the radical inversions of power that had been one of the first indicators for him of the authenticity of his experience of God. It was profoundly dispiriting for Francis that members of his own community refused to heed the very basic premises of the path of lovingkindness—a way of poverty, solidarity and mutuality that enriched the experience of being human.

It is significant that, after so much conflict and turmoil during his lifetime over how to proceed as a religious order, Francis felt compelled to make a final statement, calling those who professed loyalty to his way of life back to the place where his own journey had begun: the simple, raw and holy experience of God's love known and shared in and with the lepers. And when we recall the strict social protocols against contact with lepers discussed in the previous chapter, we see that Francis wanted nothing of the gospel's radical demand for justice and lovingkindness to the oppressed to be lost as his movement grew more and more institutionalized. In the next chapter we will explore how that love can be nurtured and cultivated in the daily practice and relational habit of tenderness.

Francis and Clare call us to create, with God and other committed and like-minded individuals, loving communities of solidarity and resistance. Communities that are capable of resisting evil, in its multitude of forms, and supporting and upholding right, loving human relations. That such loving communities must actively resist corrupting forces and even inner impulses toward lesser forms of being human is a hard lesson for those of us who want to keep love "soft" and tame its force. But a love that is "stronger than death" must have and find the wherewithal to confront abusive power, protect the innocent, dismantle systems that exploit and disable ideologies that deceive.

                                    *Gillian T.W. Ahlgren*

In light of those strong counterforces, how will we sustain and nurture that depth of love?


**FOR REFLECTION:**

How do you understand tenderness?  Can you see it as a source of strength as well as vulnerability?  As the opposite, even antidote, to hardheartedness?

Can you think of examples of Jesus's tenderness?  What does that teach us about God?  In what senses is tenderness an expression of power, and what does it teach us about power?

In what senses does solidarity strengthen us, as individuals and as a larger human community?

# 5

# Grounding Our Growth in God

For love to grow, it must be rooted deeply in relationship with God while also grounded in a community oriented to cultivating and nurturing the growth of all of its members. We have already seen elements of the kind of growth we are talking about: growth in integrity, maturity, wisdom, courage, honesty, solidarity and love. In the previous chapter, we saw how love, as it is expressed in tenderness, holds the antidote to hardness of heart. In this chapter, we will explore some of the relational practices, traditionally understood as prayer and contemplation, which give us eyes to see the world and others around us from a space of loving connection. This kind of sight fuels and grounds our ongoing metanoia, and is a manifestation of the communion that God's lovingkindness draws us into.

For some people, contemplation connotes a particular temperament they think they do not have. I do not know the number of times people have said to me things like, "I am not a contemplative; I don't have that kind of patience" or "I wouldn't know how to begin to meditate." But if we think of contemplation as an expression of love—an expression that grows more intelligent, patient, and tenacious because it proceeds from an even deeper knowledge that we are loved— then perhaps we can begin to see contemplation for what it really is: a practical, living, empowering, transforming way of life that supports and energizes us at all levels of our being. This is an inborn capacity that gets trained out of us by a world that tells us how we should think, how quickly we should make decisions, and what should inform our thought processes, tripping us up by sending us a multitude of conflicting messages about what is attractive, necessary, desirable, and important. Contemplation helps us to stay accountable to our inner wisdom, to our need for counsel, to the insights that our own experiences can provide, and to our need for discipline in order to grow.

Contemplation is, first and foremost, a disposition, a willingness to engage a process, to change and be changed. Whatever our background, we can probably appreciate the multiple benefits—to ourselves, to the people we love, and to the world around us—that contemplation offers. A contemplative person is one who never stops asking "what is real?" The contemplative person values simplicity, integrity, and relational honesty so much that nothing else really matters to them. This clarity about what truly matters manifests itself in courage, calm, warmth, and vitality as their inner access to radical love radiates outward. A contemplative community brings wisdom, discretion, inspiration, and visionary leadership into the world. Like Jesus and his earliest companions, such a community nurtures growth and calls us to be accountable to the impulses that stir us toward the common good.

Contemplation is less about leaving the world and more about becoming real. As more of us dedicate ourselves to the process of becoming authentically ourselves and sharing our giftedness with others, the world becomes a different place. Because contemplation is a relational orientation, it helps us continually evolve the forms of collaboration and care that Francis and Clare inspired and nurtured. Ultimately, contemplation is growth in love guided by the One who is love.



*Gillian T.W. Ahlgren*

As such, contemplation is a holistic engagement of the will, heart, and mind that becomes a way of life. Contemplation is, emphatically, not merely a practice, although some form of practice is critical in order to develop the mind, heart, eyes and ears to see and hear, savor, behold and attend to what is most real in the world around us. Contemplation is an integral part of the process of falling in love with the One whose love is beyond all telling. No one can fully embrace a relationship with God without contemplation. The contemplative process invites us into a transforming relationship as we literally begin to behold, experience, and apprehend the presence of God. Clare of Assisi, whose letters to Agnes of Prague constitute the grounding for our discussion of the contemplative framework for a life of love, provides a beautiful and attractive expression of the contemplative way:

> Place your mind before the mirror of eternity!
> Place your soul in the brilliance of glory!
> Place your heart in the figure of the divine substance
> and, through contemplation,
> transform your entire being into the image
> of the Godhead itself,
> so that you too may feel what friends feel
> in tasting the hidden sweetness
> that, from the beginning,
> God has reserved for all God's lovers.

(See Clare, Third Letter to Agnes in Armstrong,
*The Lady*, p. 51.)

In this chapter, we will explore the contemplative way as Clare articulates it in the form of four verbs: gaze, consider, contemplate, and imitate. (For these verbs as they are embedded in Clare's Second Letter to Agnes of Prague, see Armstrong,

*The Lady*, p. 49.) As Clare explains, the process encapsulated by these four verbs invites us into a transforming relationship as we are transformed by God's companionate gaze upon us.

Engaging more deeply our relationship with God is inherently transformative, helping us to re-shape our priorities, values, daily practices and our capacity to see ourselves and our world anew. We are changed as a direct result of the profound power and mystery of the God whose love is the very source of our being. Both Francis and Clare's regular intimacy with God was what enabled their extraordinary tenderness with others; that intimacy sensitized them to God's constant presence in the human community and empowered them to work courageously to ensure that the world around them was a fitting home, for God and for all.

Francis and Clare had experienced the reality that God is always at work within creation. Their recognition that God is love and that God has loved all things into being was the foundation of their lives, and this was an awareness that they sought to embody and share in every single encounter they had. The core of Francis and Clare's desire was to invite people into the mystery of God's love through what they did and, more importantly, through who they were—or rather, who they had become over the years of embracing relationship with God. They modeled and embodied the many ways that knowing and sharing the love of God helps us to grow and thrive together. The lessons they leave us are in themselves nothing less than revolutionary. But their revolution is not meant to remain a part of a historical legacy. It is a living example of how to grow, how to truly know God, and how to share life together. Like Jesus, they invite us to experience the God who is at the center of our being and who walks with us out of the margins of our own existence.

We have already seen that one of the most primary insights of Francis and Clare's way is that human life is meant to be deeply relational. By "relational" we mean that life is best lived in solidarity and communion with one another and with God. The most critical relationship, of course, is the relationship that exists between the individual and God, a relationship that concurrently invites us into a deeper, more holistic relationship with ourselves and others. It is likely that, like Francis, we begin the transformative process of contemplation with little true self-knowledge and little to no knowledge of God. But what we all have in common is that we can only grow into the reality of loving relationship—with God, self, and others—gradually, and in small steps: through awareness, experience, moments of insight, joyful sharing, gratitude for all that is gained in encounter, sorrow for the ways that we fall short, desire to be there for the other in trustworthy and helpful ways. All of these experiences lead us to gradually let go of lesser ways of being and motivate us to embrace more whole-heartedly a new and increasingly compelling reality. We can study how Francis and Clare cultivated relationship with God in order to glean ways to see our deepest reality, despite the darkness in the world around us.

Noting that prayer is, as Teresa of Avila described it, "nothing more than conversation with One whom we know loves us," we see that Francis engaged a trusting familiarity with God, even when he hardly knew who God was. If we go back to one of the critical moments in Francis's own conversion, we can hear again his profound prayer before the cross of San Damiano as the starting point of a life-long conversation:

> Enlighten the darkness of my heart.
> Give me a right faith, certain hope, and perfect love,
> with deep humility, wisdom and understanding,
> that I may know and do Your most holy will.

We can all relate to this prayer of a person who just needs help. If we are honest, we will admit that we all start from a place of insufficiency, even emptiness, at times. Francis's words are a simple and humble recognition that the human heart is fundamentally mysterious; elements of ourselves remain hidden and "dark" to us, and many of the human trials and tribulations we face are often exacerbated by our lack of deepest self-knowledge.

By 1205, the likely date of his San Damiano prayer, Francis probably knew that a very deep kind of illuminating prayer was necessary if he were going to know himself and embrace the way of life God might intend for him. We can see in this prayer that, just like us, Francis had no idea where the God of his heart would lead him. Surely he often returned to this humble request for guidance as his questions about how best to live out God's will for him increased. Francis's prayer to "enlighten the darkness of my heart" can be seen (and could even serve us today) as a simple mantra, repeated over and over as a daily intention to continue to turn over what is "dark" (i.e., puzzling, mysterious, challenging or even frightening or disgusting) to us into the light of God, that we might learn from it whatever God would teach us and continue, in this way, to grow in wisdom and grace and goodness. This intention to learn from all that life hands us helps transform even our most challenging times into moments that allow even deeper relationship with God.

As Francis grew in his relationship with God, we see many instances of both the spontaneity and constancy of his prayer life, suggesting that he enjoyed a deep and rich intimacy with God. But he himself tells us almost nothing. *The Legend of Three Companions* states that Francis's attraction to prayer began after his return to Assisi following his experiences as a prison of war in Perugia. The text specifically correlates an inner feeling of intense tenderness with these moments of prayer, which began in the same sudden way as Francis's initial experience of God in the leper colony:



*Gillian T.W. Ahlgren*

Suddenly Francis was visited by the Lord who filled his heart with so much tenderness that he was unable to speak or move. He could only feel and hear this marvelous tenderness; it left him so estranged from any sensation that, as he himself said later, even if he had been completely cut to pieces, he would not have been able to move… From that very hour he began to consider himself of little value and to despise those things which he had previously held in love… Often, almost daily, he withdrew secretly to pray. He was inclined to do so by that same tenderness he had tasted earlier, which now visited him ever more frequently, driving him to prayer in the piazza and in other public places. (See *The Legend of Three Companions*, 3:7-8, in Armstrong, *The Founder*, p. 72.)

Francis's actual forms of prayer were quite simple and straightforward, always reflecting a strong desire to be shown, led, drawn toward what God wanted from him. He sought solitude where, in quiet, he might better hear God's guiding voice. At critical moments he asked God for specific direction in prayer and opened scripture three times to allow the Word of God to speak to him directly with respect to the question posed. He enjoined Clare and other trusted companions to pray for and with him as he discerned God's will for him over the course of his life. He was devoted to the Eucharist and meditated on scripture. He composed and sang hymns of praise. He maintained an attitude of gratitude and love in the face of a wide range of human responses to his lifestyle. Through consideration of these regular features of Francis's life, we can appreciate this deepening dialogue with God, with and beyond words, that gradually became an intense and empowering partnership.

But these practices in and of themselves do not help us

understand, in a more "inner" way, the process by which Francis's life gradually became a single, whole and seamless, integrated prayer. Francis's prayer practice was fervent—physical as well as mental—and continuous, embedded into the fabric of his life. Bonaventure writes:

> Francis strove to keep his spirit in the presence of God by praying without ceasing so that he might not be without the comfort of his Beloved… Whether walking or sitting, inside or outside, working or resting, he was so intent on prayer that he seemed to have dedicated to it not only his heart and body but also all his effort and time. (Bonaventure, *Life of St. Francis*, 10:1 in Armstrong, *The Founder*, 605.)

Although Francis's prayer life seems to have evolved to a place in which he often experienced moments of absorption and encounter with God that suspended his ordinary activity, it was truly his perseverance in engaging contact and relationship with God that fueled his life. In light of all that we have understood about the tenderness of God's love, it is striking that many of the early commentators associate Francis's experience of prayer with a profound inner tenderness. The tenderness that Francis experienced in prayer became inseparable from the fervor of his love, which Bonaventure called "a blaze of flames that many waters could not quench." (Bonaventure, *Life of St. Francis*, 13:2 in Armstrong, *The Founder*, p. 606) As this text suggests, for Francis, as for Clare, prayer and love were a single act, a single force, a flowing energy that extended itself gracefully into every facet of daily life.

To summarize, Francis made continual recourse to his relationship with God, in wordless ways that brought alive the words of John's gospel that those who love God in Jesus and live in God's word will know the indwelling presence of God (cf. John 14:23, a passage which became critical to Teresa of Avila, especially in her *Interior Castle*). The process of becoming a dwelling place for God sacralizes our experience of self, other and world. As we begin to understand ourselves as dwelling places of God, we can then take more seriously the possibility that our life, our selfhood, and our relationships with others are all sacred spaces to be explored and nurtured.

Creating an inner space for the indwelling presence of God was so important that Francis implored his companions to prioritize above all else the practice of loving and adoring God as simply and wholeheartedly as possible:

> But, in the holy love which is God, I beg all my brothers, both the ministers and the others, after overcoming every impediment and putting aside every care and anxiety, to serve, love, honor and adore the Lord God with a clean heart and a pure mind in whatever way they are best able to do so, for that is what God wants above all else. Let us always make a home and a dwelling place there for the One Who is the Lord God Almighty. (See Francis of Assisi, *Earlier Rule*, 22:26-27 in Armstrong, *Francis: The Saint*, 80.)

Creating a dwelling place for God, a suitable home, in our hearts, our communities and our world, for the One whose love gives life, is at the very heart of the gospel way. We participate in the making of places sacred as we attend to the presence of God that already dwells there and as we open ourselves to our own graced capacity to be vessels of that presence in our world. Gathering intentionally in loving community to help one another grow creates a sacred space, and Francis and Clare model the kind of reverence and right relationship that recognize the human person as a sacred place of encounter with God.

We have discussed the importance of encounter, as well as the critical functions of solidarity and resistance, but these stages in the process of metanoia need a concrete grounding. They need a relational orientation and relational practices, with God and with one another, so that we can deliberately sacralize the ways that we accompany one another, fueling and vitalizing our simplicity, our compassionate care, and our purity of heart. No human being can sustain such qualities alone. The community that Clare developed at San Damiano can provide a profound example of how to live in ways that nurture and sustain love and how to love in ways that give life.

To return for a moment to the narrative of Francis and Clare's own life of metanoia, we can see just how pivotal San Damiano was. There Clare could pray daily before the same cross that had stirred Francis to "rebuild my home." She had a concrete reminder of God's loving invitation to change and be changed. For Clare and her sisters, the daily practice of gazing on that cross, especially when enhanced by communal prayer, scripture reading, Eucharist, and participating in the care of others, reinforced the many ways that they were sustained and fed by a living God. These daily habits fueled a process of transformation in God that they could extend into the world around them. The cross served as a mirror in which Clare could see herself as God saw her: beloved, bathed in tenderness and kindness, and aglow with the love of God.

Clare was convinced, through her own experience, that in gazing into the mirror of the cross and taking in the tenderness of the God we know in that space, we see and receive God's self-giving love, a revolutionary experience that changes all aspects of our lives. Over time, Clare's sustained awareness of the incarnate God ceased to be located solely in one place, as she felt and experienced the reality of God's effective presence in her and in the human community.

In ways that we should appropriate in our lives today, Francis and Clare model for us how to become more aware of and

                                   *Gillian T.W. Ahlgren*

attuned to God's active presence in humanity. They teach us that genuine prayer requires us to grow. Their prayer, like their lives, was not sentimental or self-serving. It was never demanding or transactional. In voicing and living their deep desire to be in synchronicity and union with God's desire for the human community, their prayer left the world tangibly better off.

Clare's fourth and final letter to Agnes of Prague, full of rich, spousal imagery, reflects her deep intimacy with God. Written shortly before her death in 1153, the letter makes clear that Clare's prayer had become an act as regular as breathing. If these letters to Agnes had not survived, we would have little insight into the method of metanoia. But Clare generously shares a way of engaging the transformative presence of God in daily life.

> Gaze upon that mirror each day,
>   O Queen and Spouse of Jesus Christ,
>     and continually study your face in it,
>       that you may adorn yourself completely,
>         within and without...
>
>           with the flowers and garments of all the virtues.

This deep and steady consideration of the constant love of God had provided Clare the supportive embrace of the one

> Whose beauty all the blessed hosts of heaven
>   unceasingly admire,
> Whose tenderness touches,
> Whose contemplation refreshes,
> Whose kindness overflows,
> Whose delight overwhelms,
> Whose remembrance delightfully dawns...

(For both of the above passages see Clare, "Fourth Letter to Agnes," 9, 11-12, in Armstrong, *The Lady*, 55)

Clare's understanding of her love relationship with God was informed by the bride in the Song of Songs. In the passage below, there are four embedded references to the life of a spouse of God (Song of Songs 1:3, 2:4, 2:6, and 1:1). Clare wants Agnes and all of us to know that we, too, can grow into the fullness of our identity as God's cherished partner when she writes:

> May you, therefore, be inflamed ever more strongly with the fire of love! As you further contemplate God's ineffable delights, riches and perpetual honors, may you cry out from the great desire and love of your heart:
>
> Draw me after you,
> let us run in the fragrance of your perfumes,
> O heavenly Spouse!
> I will run and not tire,
> until You bring me into the wine-cellar,
> until Your left hand is under my head
>   and Your right hand will embrace me happily,
> You will kiss me with the happiest kiss of Your mouth.
>
> (Clare, "Fourth Letter to Agnes" in Armstrong, *The Lady*, p. 57)

Commenting on this letter, Ilia Delio asks us to notice Clare's "youthful spirit of joy." Although Clare was nearly sixty years old and had struggled with debilitating physical illness over the course of her life, Delio notes: "Clare writes her final letter to Agnes as if in the youth of her spiritual life. She is filled with hope, love and desire, as if she has just discovered the source of happiness, the pearl of great price… A lifetime of gazing generates in Clare the Spirit of confidence in the love of God and the spiritual transformation of her own life into the image of Christ. Even at the end of her life when she was sick and frail, her spirit showed the lightness of a youth in love…" (Ilia Delio, *Clare of Assisi: A Heart Full of Love*, 97-8, 100).

                                          *Gillian T. W. Ahlgren*

Clare's mature theological vision suggests that a profound, vibrant, and fertile love relationship with God incarnates itself within us and, through us, in the larger world around us, as we gradually enter into the living and dynamic experience of God through Clare's simple method: gaze, consider, contemplate, imitate. This is a four-step, comprehensive process that becomes a transformative way of life.

Francis and Clare's relational way of life begins through the gaze. The love of God that we see extending itself toward us as we gaze at the incarnate God invites us into a new understanding, both of who God is and who we are. Gazing, as a practice and as a relational invitation, is grounded in God, but does not remain a practice between us and God alone. Gazing becomes a way to relate to others and the world around us: lovingly and with the desire to dwell together and bring the best out of one another. For to gaze is not simply to see; to gaze is to be drawn into the one whom we see.

To gaze is to behold rather than to scrutinize and examine. Gazing entails a particular attitude, disposition and presence in us that is well worth exploring. For our contemporary culture may well have stripped us of the practice of the gaze. The visual images which surround us, many of which are violent or pornographic, have dissociated our eyes from our hearts and minds, which threatens to make our vision superficial, voyeuristic, self-serving, crude, and, certainly, unloving. Forging a holistic relationship with what we see and learning to behold what is within us and around us is part and parcel of the practice of the gaze—a practice that we may not even know how to engage.

The art of gazing is a form of true beholding. The gaze, by definition, involves a disposition of reverent attention and tenderness of heart. This more open stance predisposes us to be able to learn from what we see, to be in relationship with what we see, to be transformed by what we take in from the gaze. The act of gazing is an act of the heart through the eyes, not of the eyes alone. The mind attends, too, but in reverent silence, there to ponder rather than to dissect through analysis. If we have spent enough time in nature beholding creation and natural beauty, the gaze is more natural to us. The gaze opens up a space in us to meet and be met in a transforming encounter, to share mutually in the space between or among us, and this practice is critical, both for our relationship with God and our relationship with one another.

As we bring both tenderness of heart and our full attention to the cross of San Damiano—a cross that neither emphasizes nor ignores suffering, reflecting more prominently the kind eyes and loving embrace Christ extends into the world—we may begin to sense the open arms of God who comes to us there, to meet and be met. We join the cloud of witnesses surrounding Jesus on the San Damiano cross, and we enter a relational space that suspends time. Clare asks Agnes (and us) to gaze upon the cross as in a mirror because that gaze of lovingkindness helps us to know ourselves inwardly, to glimpse and engage who we can become. Once we are graced with the vision of ourselves that God gives us, that same gaze can open in us the desire to become that person, in partnership with the One who calls that personhood out of us. This deepening happens as we proceed to the second verb in Clare's four-step method, "consider."

Consideration brings reflection into the relationship that has been entered into through the gaze. If the gaze emphasizes the heart, consideration then joins our intellectual capacities with our affective ones. We do not stop gazing when we start considering, but considering helps us to integrate the intellect with the heart from a loving space of greater focused attention. Consideration refines the gaze by centering it in



*Gillian T. W. Ahlgren*

a space of single-mindedness, setting aside anything that can alter or weaken our gaze and integrating knowledge, awareness, contextual understanding, and other dimensions of human insight into who or what we are gazing at.

Consideration can also be understood as encompassing our desire and willingness to enter into another person's reality— the next step as we behold them—and to let that reality touch us, inform us, and sensitize us. Consideration helps us both to add a process of knowing to the gaze and to correct some of our lesser forms of knowing according to what we learn through the eyes and experience of the one who is beheld. Consideration helps us, as beholders, to enter more deeply into the practical corollaries to loving relationship. Consideration prepares us for deeper, more concrete expressions of relational love. But before we are ready for effective action, we need both the space of consideration and contemplation, to come. By integrating intellect and affect, consideration allows us to stand committedly in a space of love and aspiring wisdom. From this integrated space, contemplative engagement, the third step, is possible.

Contemplation requires a considerable shift within us, but we have been prepared for that shift by the previous two steps of gazing and considering, allowing us to gain the relational perspective that contemplation provides. Roch Niemier explains this shift simply, saying that contemplation is not so much a method or practice, but an awareness: an awareness "that it is God who is contemplating us." This possibility is so profound that Niemier asks us to repeat this formula to ourselves, over and over, encouraging us to consider that, in our contemplative prayer, we and God meet:

One definition of prayer might be: Prayer is God praying in us. The God who lives in you and me prays in you and me. This frees us and is so right because it allows God to be

God. Contemplation is not what I do, or what I do to God. It is what God does in and with me through an invitation to intimacy and union. (Niemier, *In the Footsteps*, p. 117)

Here is the corrective to our worry that prayer or contemplation is something that we have to accomplish—and that we are unable to do very well. If prayer is truly, in part, God praying in us, then contemplation is the awareness of, consent to, and participation in the aliveness of God in us. Contemplation is the grounding for us to learn how to collaborate with the divine in every facet of our lives. Contemplation is the space in which we learn not only God's aliveness but God's desire to make us partners with God in the work of making the world a better place. In this sense, there is no true tension between contemplation and action. The contemplative life moves toward prophetic action, and the active life craves the contemplative grounding that is so necessary for all that we do in the world around us.

The fourth verb in Clare's process, "imitate," brings this point home. For in Clare's schema, imitation does not mean to mimic the behavior of another. As Roch Niemier develops this term, he explains:

When Clare used the term [imitation], she was asking Agnes to become the image of the God on whom she gazed… Imitation is transformation insofar as Christ comes alive in my life. In this transformation contemplative union happens… as we give ourselves over to the truth of "God contemplating me," God's gaze of love over the course of years transforms us and empowers us. Eventually, God slowly recognizes God's own image in us. It is important to think of this process in terms of relationships and the wholly mystery of growing in love. I personally am not sure anyone can truly pray without being in love. (Niemier, *In the Footsteps*, pp. 118-20).

What Niemier helps us to see is that we ourselves are transformed in large part because we now actively engage a relationship that empowers us. The only work involved in contemplation is our openness to the transforming activity of God's love in us. This relationship gives us a unitive strength and a wisdom that is beyond what we can acquire on our own. We become conscious of God's presence alive and active within us, healing us, gentling us, liberating us, and strengthening us. The relationship with God formed through contemplation gives us the capacity for purposeful action in the world around us:

> When we look at prayer this way we become not only transformed but empowered, and being so empowered, we are able to work to effect the necessary changes in ourselves, in life, and in society and the world around us. God works in union with us, with our spirit, not apart from us. It is a matter of working at life together. (Niemier, *In the Footsteps*, p. 120)

The scriptural and theological grounding for this deep inner reality is the image of God in which we are said to be created (Genesis 1:26-27) but which has been clouded over, perhaps even effaced, through our estrangement from God. Actively engaging that relationship with God, guided by Christ's instructive example of incarnate love and empowered by the living Spirit of God, creates a space for the indwelling presence of God which Francis had exhorted his followers to seek: "Let us always make a home and a dwelling place… for the One Who is the Lord God Almighty." (Francis of Assisi, *Earlier Rule*, 22: 27, in Armstrong, *The Saint*, 80.)

This approach to God may well take some time for us to acknowledge, understand, accept and integrate. The images we have of God—whether they emphasize severity and judgment, mystery and remoteness, ethereality and transcendence, or power and grandeur and majesty—may keep us from entering into a realm of intimacy, familiarity, and genuine partnership and collaboration with God. Let me clarify that, by growing in love toward intimacy with the One who loves us, we are not discarding God's mystery, transcendence, power or majesty. In fact, to know that a God who transcends our understanding still wants familiar, collaborative relationship ought only to increase our awe and wonder. Further, intimacy with God does not lead us away from an invested engagement with our world; it shows us more clearly how and where we may be instruments of the life-giving love that we come to know more deeply from its Source.

Time with God transforms us and gives us a similarly keen and vital interest in the condition and health of creation. To gaze at the human community is to see a spectrum of behaviors, many of which clearly cannot please God. Gazing, considering and contemplating the profound injustices in our world leads us to embrace and imitate all the more strongly the counter-strategy of life-giving love. Or, as a friend of mine said simply, "Once we get to know God, we don't want to let God down." God's tender love for each of us makes it impossible for God to disregard the egregious ways that we treat one another and our earth. Grief, indignation, outrage, and a constant call to conversion are also a part of God's loving relationship with humankind. Francis and Clare's sensitivity to God's pathos had them constantly preaching, by word and by example, the radical simplicity and self-stripping necessary to begin to remediate the injustices in our world and to model God's solidarity with those left behind.

Each of us is called into this kind of deepening relationship with God that sensitizes us to who, in God, we can become. Henri Nouwen opens up the reality of this relational exchange, this continual back-and-forth between us and God in a way that may be easier for us to appreciate. In The Life of the Beloved, Nouwen writes:

                                     *Gillian T.W. Ahlgren*

The unfathomable mystery of God is that God is a lover who wants to be loved. The one who created us is waiting for our response to that love that gave us our being. God not only says: "You are my Beloved." God also asks: "Do you love me?" and offers us countless chances to say "Yes." That is the spiritual life: the chance to say "Yes" to our inner truth. (Henri Nouwen, *Life of the Beloved*, p. 133.)

But this ongoing dialogue with God is not just a personal one. As Nouwen explains, the same God who calls us beloved also comes alive in us as a Spirit of love giving us collective opportunities to create a more humane and just world.

The spiritual life counteracts the countless divisions that pervade our daily life and cause destruction and violence. These divisions are interior as well as exterior: the divisions among our most intimate emotions and the divisions among the most widespread social groupings. The division between gladness and sadness within me or the division between the races, religions and cultures around me all find their source in the diabolic forces of darkness. The Spirit of God, the Spirit that calls us the Beloved, is the Spirit that unites and makes whole. There is no clearer way to discern the presence of God's Spirit than to identify the movements of unification, healing, restoration, and reconciliation. Whenever the Spirit works, divisions vanish and inner as well as outer unity manifests itself. (Nouwen, *Life of the Beloved*, p. 135)

*　　*　　*

Through the gaze of love we gain a whole new understanding of self, of God, and of other; this understanding is in no way abstract. It is a life-giving, transformative understanding, a "saving knowledge" taken lovingly into the whole of our being, such that we are left changed, different, enhanced, and empowered by it—empowered for joy, empowered for new life, given a new sense of purpose, a true reason for being here on earth. How can it be otherwise if gazing is actually also an experience of scripture's invitation to "taste and see" the goodness of God? As Clare so beautifully expresses it, in the process of this gaze we "taste the hidden sweetness that God has reserved for those who love God." (Clare of Assisi, "Third Letter to Agnes of Prague," 14, in Armstrong, *The Lady*, 51.) Clare's way shows us that the "gospel life" is not grandiose or exaggerated, either in its leadership or in its servitude. It is thoroughly and genuinely relational. It eschews pageantry. It is a simple and humble and joyful creation of a dwelling place for the divine—the making of a space for God's presence, in our hearts, our homes, our communities, and our troubled world.

The constancy of the demands of our world requires our dedication to sustaining the gaze and allowing the insights gained there to inspire us to right action. The gaze is a living, dynamic experience of God that we take into ourselves and live back out into the world. In our hearts, our bodies, our homes, and our communities, this lived relationship with God takes form and shape and more concrete expression. Thus, as we participate more actively in the gaze, we are graced to become part of the ongoing incarnation of the living God. Not only do we make God's love more palpable and real to our contemporaries, but we also model the possibility of deeper partnership and collaboration with God, so that the love of God might be made more manifest in human history.

An integral part of the gaze itself is sustaining it, which is far more difficult to do than we might think, particularly when the messages of the world around us strongly contradict what we take

                                   *Gillian T.W. Ahlgren*

in through the gaze of God's lovingkindness. Using the gaze as our core practice of prayer and our point of entry into deepening relationship includes the ways that we position ourselves so that we can sustain the gaze. There are too many things—in ourselves, in our lives, even in the intimate spheres of our lives, much less in our world—that can easily and powerfully get in the way of the gaze. Acknowledging this vulnerability, in us and in the human condition at large, can remind us not to allow anything that contradicts God's loving gaze to detain us from a space at God's side, wrapped in the embrace that shows us who we are.

A principled commitment to sustaining the gaze is perhaps all the more important as we are learning the practice of the gaze, for there is so much to learn and apprehend and integrate through the gaze. As we dedicate ourselves to Clare's four-fold practice, much of what orders our lives will begin to show signs of inadequacy or falsity, in comparison to what comes to us through the gaze of God's love. It is worth remembering that Francis and Clare gave up all they had in order to approach God's gaze simply and nakedly. It is for God to show us the new norms of our life-with-God, and this will likely result in profound change on our part. But it will be change that brings a greater lightness of being and a deepening fruitfulness in us. Our culture all but demands that we conform to lives that lack deepest joy, vitality, and love. And sometimes we ourselves settle into joyless lives, in the name of responsibility, duty, and doing what we think we "should" be doing. My own sense is that such confusion and even spiritual self-deprivation come from our not lifting up everything to God in prayerful conversation and taking our cues about all of the details of our lives directly from the sacred, unitive space of the gaze. Recall Roch Niemier's frank appraisal: "I personally am not sure anyone can truly pray without being in love." I am always heartened when I remember Teilhard de Chardin's simple indicator that we are on the right path when he writes: "Joy is the infallible sign of the Spirit of God."

Our lives, because they are human, will contain experiences and events that disrupt the gaze and perhaps even threaten to dislodge our engaged apprehension of God's love. Approaching God from a space of deep simplicity and openness—one in which we come without trying to force an outcome or bring too much with us into the space of encounter—supports the healing and transformation that God's love makes possible. Ilia Delio captures the delicacy of this process when she writes:

> Gazing requires a space within the heart to receive what we see and to "embrace" what we see. Poverty helps create this space because when we are free of things we possess or that possess us we are able to see more clearly and to receive what we see within us. (Ilia Delio, *Clare of Assisi*, p. 31)

That the things we possess can "possess us," as Delio says above, doesn't always occur to us. But this was precisely the insight that propelled Francis and Clare into their way of life. Through them we can more easily see that so often our lives in the material world have holds on us that we do not appreciate. We gain a far greater freedom to make choices toward the deeper flourishing of our lives and our relationship with God in the engaged space of the gaze.

We have acknowledged before that the gaze of God that we sustain is not just given for us alone; it strengthens us for our work in the world around us. We must be faithful and attentive to the cherishing love that God's gaze teaches us, sustaining the gaze so that we can learn to gaze upon ourselves and gaze out upon others and the world in the same loving ways that we are being taught.

We might conclude by suggesting that the gaze is a "movement toward"—a movement toward God, toward the authentic self, toward the image of God embedded within us and, through the creative process, within all that God loved and loves into being. While its context is silence and reverence as we behold, the gaze itself is not passive. It is a holistic movement of the heart—an impulse of love within us, made possible by the impetus and embrace of God's love, which empowers the heart to "open its arms,' so to speak, to allow the Spirit of God's love to enter." (See Ilia Delio, *Clare of Assisi*, p. 31)

What happens to us, in us, when the Spirit of God's love enters our hearts? We can see things in an entirely new way. We see with clarity. We can see ourselves as God sees us—potentially free of that which hinders us and keeps us from knowing and manifesting the image of God within us. We can also see, within ourselves and within humanity, the habits, practices and beliefs that keep us mired down and engaged in lesser, even degrading ways of being. This clarity enkindles a greater resolve within us and a deeper prayer for the grace to change our ways. We can see the natural world around us, alive and glowing not only with beauty but also with the light of God's love embedded within it. We develop a stronger desire to live compatibly and companionably with the natural world, in ways that sustain its beauty and spontaneous generosity. And we are overwhelmed by the generosity of love we continually discover in the God who extends this love into as much of our being as we will allow. Gradually this generous, spontaneous, humble and joyful way of life becomes part and parcel of who we are, just as it did for Francis and Clare.

"We are created to express the Word of God in our lives," Ilia Delio asserts. "In fact," she continues,

> without striving for such a goal, we remain incomplete and lost, ambivalent, restless and anxious. What Clare calls us to is not something other than what we are but rather what we truly are created to be—icons of Christ. Christ lives in us

and becomes our life when we come to live our true identity (or self) in God. To put on Christ is to allow God to take root in our hearts and put on our flesh, not hiding God in the little pockets of our hearts but rather allowing the grace of God to shine through our lives—fragile and weak though they may be. (Ilia Delio, *Clare of Assisi*, p. 72)

For both Francis and Clare, life in God was "a perpetual deepening of union in love." Their example invites us to explore God's invitation be drawn ever more deeply toward the infinite source of love. Ilia Delio observes that Clare was "drawn by the infinite love of God toward happiness, fulfillment and immense joy. There is light and levity in her pursuit of holiness, as if each discovery of God's immense love is a new beginning." (Ilia Delio, *Clare of Assisi*, p. 72.)

The practice of Clare's four-step method fuels a process of transformation that leaves no part of us untouched, unchanged. While it takes place in the inner depths of our hearts, it is a transformation that completely redefines how we see and relate to ourselves, the world, and one another. As we linger in the gaze of God's love, we slowly create a deeper space for God's indwelling presence in us and in our world. This is a personal and intimate process for each of us, as we slowly apprehend that we are lovable (whether or not we have been well loved in our own lifetimes), that we are made for love, by love, and that we are meant to share that love with others. Taking this reality into ourselves, we find, perhaps to our surprise, that we have, literally, fallen in love, and the practice of this method helps us to stay in love for the rest of our lives. I am privileged to see this process of "falling in love" happen for people, over and over, as I lead them in the footsteps of Francis and Clare to Assisi through the gentle space of San Damiano and deep into the heart of La Verna.

                                    *Gillian T.W. Ahlgren*

Acquiring a growing familiarity with God's love may not be quite so common an experience for all readers of this work. Throughout this chapter, I have been speaking about God's love as if it means something to you, and yet it might be that you have never really considered that love in a deeply experiential and holistic way. Since this love is the source of life and the impetus for all meaningful change, it cannot remain abstract. If God's love is not yet, for you, a subjective reality, it occurs to me to ask you the question that the process of writing about the gaze has required me to ask of myself: "What does God's love feel like to you?" This question, coupled with the even more critical prayer that God might teach us, directly, what life-giving love is, should guide our daily lives. And yet conversations about the ways that we know God's love in our lives are rare. In the context of spiritual direction, we might be encouraged to "notice God's presence" in our lived experience, but we rarely speak of our actual and direct experiences of God's love—a living, transformative reality that, as we come to trust it, makes all the difference in our lives.

Staying in subjective contact with God's love—recalling it when our senses are dulled and doing all we can to maintain the living flame of love in our hearts—is an essential part of the journey of life. It is well worth our time to reflect on God's love daily and remember the familiar qualities of the love that gives life, so that it becomes our point of reference and constantly informs who we are becoming. Reflecting on God's love helps us recognize God's constancy, even in moments when we are overwhelmed or laid low by the challenges of life. In the moments when contemplation seems too difficult, gazing and considering is always possible, and those practices can lift our perceptions and spirits from wherever life has laid them toward the source of life. We shortchange ourselves (and those we love) when we do not explore, concretely and deeply, what God's love feels like and is capable of doing in us. Integrating that love into our daily lives is an integral part of reclaiming our humanity.

*　　*　　*

*San Damiano is one of the most peaceful places on earth. Francis built it by hand, stone by stone, as his first act of fidelity to God. Then he lovingly turned it over to Clare and the Poor Ladies as the movement to "rebuild my home" began to spread. The place still breathes the holiness of a sincere and prayerful heart. One of the greatest joys is to arrive there very early in the morning; one is entranced by the birds, the natural beauty, the simple mystery of a new day.*

*When we walk in the footsteps of Francis and Clare, we visit San Damiano twice. We fold our first visit into the drama of Francis and Clare's conversion as one step in their emerging commitment to poverty, simplicity and a gospel-centered way. Then, halfway through our journey, we return to the peace of San Damiano to explore what life in the spacious abundance on the other side of all that renunciation really feels like. On the second visit we walk there, usually in silence. The way down to San Damiano from the city center gets narrower and more peaceful with each step. Passing through the city walls and crossing the road that rings the city, one enters the shimmering grove of olive trees, and, about halfway down the hill, there is a circular area of benches. We pause to read Clare's letter to Agnes of Prague and reflect on the core steps of the transformative way, encapsulated in her counsel:*

   Most noble Queen,
     gaze,
       consider,
         contemplate
           desiring to imitate Your Spouse.

	*Gillian T.W. Ahlgren*

*When we arrive at San Damiano we proceed directly into the chapel where we follow the counsel of Clare: just gazing at the cross with quiet attentiveness, open to the presence of God without an agenda, without even words to get in the way. This contemplative gaze of love allows God to "draw out what is best in us and speak to us in loving personal terms, so that we go away from prayer a transformed person and we discover in ourselves the image God has always wanted us to be." (Roch Niemier, **In the Footsteps**, p. 116.)*

*It is not all that hard, through that contemplative gaze of love, to begin to think differently about the words Francis first absorbed here: "Francis, rebuild my home. Can't you see it's falling into ruins?" To see that this invitation was not only about rebuilding the church of San Damiano itself or even the church more broadly, as a structure and an institutional body, so much as it is about the way God invites us to be remade in love, personally and relationally. God invites us to truly become a human family by honoring, revering, nurturing and sustaining the presence of God in ourselves and in our midst.*

*Francis and Clare help us to move deeply into the heart of what "community" truly means. By eloquently teaching us how to love God passionately, in one another and in ourselves, they invite us into a new way of being. A new way of being human, a new way of being us and a new way of interacting with others, of being a people. By searching for God in true poverty, of body and of spirit, Francis and Clare found deepest freedom and joy in going right straight to the heart of things—to the very heart of God. Their way demonstrates that what we call "church" or "religion" or "spirituality" is nothing other, and should be nothing other, than the commitment to act lovingly, to live daily in the ways that God asks of us, and to develop the unique collaborative partnership with God that each of us is called to embody in the world.*

*Time at San Damiano encourages a deeper trust in the possibility of the mystical life, not as some abstract ideal for saints but as a way of life open to each of us—a way of life that would bring far more vitality and joy than any other way of life we could embrace. We are created to know, to be changed by, and to share the love of God in our lives. The gaze into God we gain at San Damiano makes that completely believable.*



*Gillian T. W. Ahlgren*

**FOR REFLECTION:**

What aspects of prayer and contemplation as they are introduced in this chapter were new to you? Which did you find particularly helpful?

Does this chapter help you make sense of the concept and practice of "contemplation in action"? If so, in what ways?

What do you make of the chapter's assertion that contemplation is inherently relational?

How do you experience your relatedness to others in the ordinary facets of life? How would you like your experience of relationships to change, and what practices can you adopt to cultivate greater sensitivity and depth in those relationships?

**6**

# A Process for Change:
# The Invitation for Today

Francis and Clare's path of metanoia offers us a viable way to engage the changes that we and our world need. Their genius was their sincerity and integrity. They were honest about their growing sense that something was missing from their lives and something rather desperately wrong was happening in their society. They allowed themselves to feel a restless inner stirring for a different way, guided by their intuitive sense of God's presence in the world around them. As they experienced that presence in the midst of human vulnerability, they knew that they could not carry on in a world that denied the inherent dignity and worth of their sisters and brothers. Committing themselves wholeheartedly to the love of God, they lived in radical solidarity with those at the margins. This way of life gave them keen and continuing insight into the ways that the human community needed to change. Their passionate desire to be instruments of love and peace led them to rid themselves and their communities of any barriers that might hinder love's capacity to reach and transform others. Their growing embodiment of God's immense love released an energy into the world through the frail but powerful channel of human presence. Their commitment to attending to God's presence in the world around them sparked a revolution that continues to offer a way forward for us today.

Francis and Clare's way is powerful, authentic and compelling, because it was forged, step by step, by simple, sincere people collaborating with others to make the world a place for all to flourish. Their twin commitments—a refusal to compromise human dignity in the face of malice and injustice and a profound dedication to embodying goodness and love—contain a vital key for our flourishing today. Francis and Clare invite us to commit to upholding the holiness of humanity, without compromise. This means that every time we see a case of marginalization, oppression, or suffering, we defend human dignity. Every time we see greed, exploitation, and violence, we hold one another ethically accountable. They invite us today into a greater intentionality in how we live together. They ask us to become a community of mutual accountability in which we scrutinize our assumptions and behaviors, aligning them with the demands of justice, dignity and peace. Where there is blindness, stubbornness, or contempt for what is good and right and just, this community does not hesitate to correct in love, denouncing all that dehumanizes us and challenging us to change behaviors and systems that exclude or oppress.

Francis and Clare ask us to become a human community that values and supports ethical and relational maturation; a community that celebrates the diversity of gifts within its members, recognizing that each person has something to contribute, building up the goodness and integrity of each of its members as well as of its collective whole. They ask us to become a community that continues to be scandalized enough by injustice that we can stand up with dignity and not only demand change but model what a genuine, life-enhancing human community looks like.

There is a true danger in becoming numb in the face of inequality and impunity, as we are forced to witness violations of human rights and human dignity now increasingly normalized in our cultures and societies. It is worth remembering that such violations constitute a genuine moral injury, to those who suffer them as well as, secondarily, to those who witness them and feel their own impotence in changing unjust situations. The growth of destitution, starvation, and lack of safety and stability in broad sectors of the world must cause more than simply fear, blame, and paralysis. We must respond with a new vision of life, an illuminating, loving way that creates possibility for all to flourish.

Although we may find the challenges of our world overwhelming, we do not have to forge a way forward from scratch. Francis and Clare can guide our vision and our practice. We, too, can seek God in the concrete ways that Francis and Clare did: through encounter and conversion, which then lead to solidarity, collaboration and communion. In fact, from their own lives, we can derive four concrete steps toward the changes that our planet and the human family cry out for us to make.

In this chapter we will return to the method articulated by Clare of Assisi in the four verbs, to engage both a genuine relationship with God and right relationship with all of creation. Returning to those verbs, we see the value of gazing daily, in love, solidarity, and lament, at one person, situation or group who is trampled down by human malice, greed, privilege, indifference, persecution or violence. Informed by genuine encounters with those who have been trampled, we can consider their experience and the circumstances that permit such violation of our dignity. We can ask God for the love, wisdom and strength to manifest the abiding love of God in their situations, and we can, with God, stand in solidarity with the persecuted and work for the transformation of human conditions that offend God.

If we are clear that we need "another way," we will need a concrete method for this way. Integrating the insights of

Francis and Clare into this method we can propose a way to engage four concrete steps in a process of metanoia that can transform us and our world. Francis and Clare's way of deeper human authenticity, integrity, fidelity, solidarity and life-giving love begins as we decide to live as sisters and brothers, sharing life together, and it consists of four simple steps.


## STEP 1:
### Gazing: a Long, Loving Look at the Real

We begin by gazing honestly and lovingly at our world and taking stock, allowing ourselves to feel the pain that comes from the many ways that we "fail to live together well." (as Nouwen, cited above, put it). Recalling that Clare's understanding of the gaze is ultimately a way to relate to others and the world around us with the desire to dwell together and bring the best out of one another, we take a thorough, quiet look at ourselves and our social reality, scanning it for what is working well, leading to God's deepening life in us and in our world, and what is not. In this "long, loving look at the real," we take time to notice deeply all that we see. If we are truly honest about the state of our world today—its global inequities, the levels of violence and instability, and the situation of the displaced, the hungry, the isolated, the trafficked, and the abandoned, how many of us can take real pride in it? The humility that can and ought to emerge in the face of the urgency and cruelty of our global reality can lead us to a "healthy unease" about who we are becoming. Francis and Clare ask us to gaze at our world in order to become wiser and more caring about how we are in relationship to it. Our relational commitment, to God and to others, is the most critical expression of who we are and is the ultimate criterion on which our lives will be judged.


Concern for others must be expressed individually and socially, not just as "charity" to an individual but as social change, as a

                    *Gillian T.W. Ahlgren*

"constant and healthy unease" in a "world where some revel, spend with abandon and live only for the latest consumer goods, even as others look on from afar, living their entire lives in abject poverty." (Pope Francis, *The Call to Holiness in Today's World*, pars. 99 and 101.) Prioritizing this relational response to the dignity of the other will ultimately require us to say no to many things in our world. As we engage this challenging inventory, we should be as uncompromising as Francis and Clare were, both in our commitment to our sisters and brothers and in our determination to move to a place of honesty and right relationship. Although the cultural norms that they rejected may be somewhat different from the ones that we shall have to reject today, they remind us of the fortitude we will need, both to seek God and to reject what is not of God. In the depths of that honesty, it is likely that we will also recognize our need for one another, as trustworthy collaborators in the word of loving the world into a better place.

This space of greater honesty will give us new awarenesses about the many ways that our way of life routinely denies the rights, the voices, and even the presence of many in our world who have a great deal to contribute. To gaze around the tables of our corporate, governmental, economic and even religious institutions will require us to acknowledge that the majority of people on this planet still live without access to influence, power or even ways of communicating the extremes of poverty and suffering within the human community. Those who are excluded are excluded to our own detriment, since their active experience of what is not working in our world provides important insight into how we must change.

## STEP 2:

### Considering through Encounter and Reflection

Having gazed carefully at our current reality, we engage a genuine encounter with others who will take us to the core of what troubles us in what we have seen. In the second step, deliberately-engaged encounters at the margins help us to learn more about the social reality—the places of suffering and need, the places of scandal and injustice, the ways that God's people need support and encouragement, the places where new life can spring forth, the ways that our systems and structures, habits and patterns need to change. In Clare's schema of "gaze, consider, contemplate and imitate," encounter becomes a way of truly considering the reality of others that we have glimpsed through the gaze.

As Francis and Clare teach us, solidarity is rooted in transforming encounters that give God a chance to speak to us through the challenges of our time and the poor who show us God's face. It is through our common humanity that the incarnate God comes to meet us, freeing us from the chains of an individualistic, indifferent, and self-centered mentality, in order to "attain a way of living and thinking which is more humane, noble and fruitful, and which will bring dignity to our presence on this earth." (Pope Francis, *On Care for Our Common Home*, par. 14). Encountering God in our sisters and brothers and finding, in their stories, points of entry into our own humanity is gripping, compelling and exactly what Pedro Arrupe captures in his poem about falling in love and staying in love. The love that gives meaning to our lives is revealed to us as we discover that we have the capacity to be there for others, to be there with others in their space of deepest need. As Alan Jones helped us to understand what happened to Francis when he first discovered God in the leper colony: "This God is no hobby."

Francis and Clare teach us that the lens of poverty gives us a privileged view of the presence of God. But poverty is not simply a means to see God; poverty provides us with a new honesty about our human limitations. Poverty is the recognition that, in and of ourselves, each of us is insufficient. This disposition of humility opens us to the constant surprise of God's presence

   *Gillian T.W. Ahlgren*

and activity in our midst. Our orientation to the suffering poor in a world of violence and injustice attunes us to "the saving power at work in their lives" and, as Pope Francis reminds us, "we need to let ourselves be evangelized by them," embracing "the mysterious wisdom which God wishes to share with us through them." (Pope Francis, *Joy of the Gospel*, par. 198)

The realities of our world, the compelling cry of the poor, a cry that God hears, even when we do not, ask us to seek both the grace of tears to weep and the grace of strength to act. These graces are part and parcel of the third step of contemplation in Clare's method. We look, with God, at reality, asking for the gift to be more sensitive to what is happening all around us and "the courage to respond to this reality, to arise and take it firmly in hand" and to respond firmly to those who "devour the innocence of our children":

An innocence robbed from them by the oppression of illegal slave labor, prostitution and exploitation. An innocence shattered by wars and forced immigration, with the great loss that this entails. Thousands of our children have fallen into the hands of gangs, criminal organizations and merchants of death, who only devour and exploit their neediness… We live in a world where almost half of the children who die under the age of five do so because of malnutrition. According to the most recent report presented by UNICEF, unless the world situation changes, in 2030 there will be 167 million children living in extreme poverty, 69 million children under the age of five will die between 2016 and 2030, and 16 million children will not receive basic schooling.

Asking us to consider the challenging realities of our world today and the counter-narrative that God's love invites in us, Pope Francis concludes with poignant and critical questions for us today: "Can we truly experience Christian joy if we turn our backs on these realities?  Can Christian joy even exist if we ignore the cry of our brothers and sisters, the cry of the children?" (See Pope Francis, *Letter to the Bishops on the Feast of the Holy Innocents*, December 28, 2016.)  The God who speaks to us in the suffering of our sisters and brothers asks us to act upon what we learn as we gaze, consider, and contemplate this suffering in our world today.

Relationship with that God will require us to make choices, and we need an overarching principle to guide those choices.  Francis and Clare teach us to remain uncompromisingly faithful to growing into our partnership with God and living as a community in union with God's dream for us and for our world.  The gospel invitation to new life is a call to a new way of seeing reality and a whole new identity in which we are truly sister and brother to all.  Each of us is called into covenantal relationship with God, and together we are called to become a community sensitized by the stories and needs of the marginalized, deeply committed to eradicating exclusion and living as a people.  Over the course of his pontificate Pope Francis modeled this way of life, a profound way of relating to one another that facilitates our discovering God in the messiness of our own midst.  And he told us quite frankly that we have little other choice but to figure out how to live together well—justly, generously, responsibly, and joyfully:

Any Christian community, if it thinks it can comfortably go its own way without concern and effective cooperation in helping the poor to live with dignity and reaching out to everyone, will also risk breaking down, however much it may talk about social issues or criticize governments.  It will easily drift into a spiritual worldliness camouflaged by religious practices, unproductive meetings and empty talk. (Pope Francis, *Joy of the Gospel*, par. 207)

                                    *Gillian T.W. Ahlgren*

The message for the committed Christian today is clear: we are called to grow into our God-centered identity, and, as we do, we will be called upon to make choices. Each and every choice must be made toward the flourishing of our collaborative partnership with God. As Clare points out to Agnes, any attempt to name or define ourselves in terms other than the most directly God-centered ones, can easily "hinder us" or be a "stumbling block" and must be rejected as a source of complacency or even self-deception.


## STEP 3:
### Deepening our Relationship with God
### through Contemplation and Colloquy


We will not be able to know God in our midst without engaging fruitfully the third step of our process: colloquy and contemplation. This third step allows the grace of deepening relationship with God to operate in and through us. We dedicate deliberate time and space with God to engage loving partnership with God in all areas of our lives. This stage may begin with a reflective lifting up with God what we have seen and experienced. The colloquial dimensions of our prayer allow us to share with God at all levels, even as we listen and leave space for deepening insight. The contemplative dimensions give God room to take greater shape in us. Empowered by our relationship with God, we are more able to see God's face, understand the invitation of the suffering and resurrected One, and follow the promptings of the Spirit.


But our aspiration to image God in the world around us is not, and cannot be, solely an individual pursuit. Our communities, too, must radiate the reality of God's presence. We are called to embrace our individuality and our relatedness in ways that sacralize us and our world. This will require a process of growth, maturation and grace. As Parker Palmer writes:

What we need is not simply the individual at prayer, seeking to stand in his or her own sacred space. We need a corporate practice that seeks a space in which we can all stand together. We need to know that God wants to bring us together as God's people and that we must listen to each other, in the words and in the silences between them, testing our own truth against the truth received by others. We need to know that God will work a greater truth in all of us standing together than can be worked in any one of us standing alone. (Parker Palmer, *The Promise of Paradox*, pp. 91-2.)

The challenges to us in an era as oriented to consumption and conspicuous waste are obvious. Simply the clarity to see that more isn't always better can be revelatory. This gravitation toward "more" infects people from corporate boardrooms to middle-class families to pastoral staff meetings. We are hardly immune to the cultural force and momentum of such a worldview, making Francis and Clare's radical embrace of poverty completely freeing for us today. Not only does it liberate us from too much stuff and the stresses of having to take care of stuff, our movement to radical simplicity begins to cut the cords of injustice that link production and consumption to unjust wages, trafficking in persons, exploitation of resources, contamination of our water supplies and lands through the use of unnecessary chemicals, unhealthy means of extraction, or inadequate practices of sustainable production and disposal. Although many of us may be deeply concerned about the state of our planet, the plight of the displaced, or the situation of those who suffer injustice, most of us are also complicit in what we lament because the structural and cultural forces that rely on exploitation and exclusion in order to thrive permeate nearly all levels of our daily life. At the same time, it is easier than ever to turn away from unjust suffering, to insulate ourselves from the legitimate demands of our sisters and brothers for

	*Gillian T.W. Ahlgren*

solidarity, inclusion, and the same rights to dream, to create, and to collaborate that so many of us are squandering. Committing ourselves to encounters and projects that build interpersonal, intergenerational and intercultural solidarity is a critical way for us to know, experientially, that we belong to one another and to learn how to collaborate in the flourishing of our world.

Francis and Clare loved God the way God should be loved—wholeheartedly. Each person's wholehearted love of God may take different form or shape, but we have no real excuse for withholding love from God, to whom we owe our very being. If we are unsure how to love God, we can start simply and slowly, by bringing the whole of ourselves to God: our concerns, the things that trouble and challenge us, the things in our lives and our world that simply aren't right. We can start simply, by fixing our gaze upon the world around us, in its beauty and in its suffering, in order "to become painfully aware, to dare to turn what is happening to the world into our own personal suffering and thus to discover what each of us can do about it." (Pope Francis, *On Care for Our Common Home*, par. 19.)

We ourselves routinely turn away from the mystery and beauty of God's creation—especially God's indwelling presence within all that God has created—and need to commit ourselves to a direct and attentive relationship with all of creation. The mystery of a seed coming to life, growing into a plant, and subsequently providing food for us is increasingly hard to appreciate when we receive our food, vacuum-packed, from a freezer somewhere. Nor can we sense our responsibility for the quality of the soil it comes from, the cleanliness of the water that supports its growth, or any of the ways that we are directly related to all that is. The grace of meal sharing and community building slowly disappears as we grow accustomed to picking up a meal from a drive-through and wolfing it down in our automobile on the way to the next errand. Is such a way of life really viable, especially as we now see its life-crushing corollaries?  Plastic water bottle after plastic water bottle now churning into water supplies and food chains as toxic nanoparticles that threaten both biodiversity and the well-being of species all the way up the line to human beings.  The movement to produce massive amounts of pork and beef for human consumption contributing to toxic levels of soil and water contamination and greenhouse gas emissions.  The throwaway culture that has extended itself strongly into the human community, as we consider more and more of its members expendable.

We are blinded to the beauty that permeates our world when we are not in direct contact with its contours, landscapes, elements, and species, and when our habits of extraction and consumption are not revealed in all of their lethal toxicity.  We deceive ourselves when we turn away from the negative, even devastating, impacts of our daily habits.  Each careless practice fits into a larger jigsaw puzzle of deception, until we are so blinded by "the way things are" that we can see neither their falsity nor the many ways that humans have created a reality for themselves that is entirely other than what God invites us into.  The reality of God, which is the reality that Francis and Clare invite us to explore, is a realm of peace and abundance, and it is rooted in communities of sharing and graced generosity.

Toward the end of his life, wracked by pain and blind from trachoma, Francis composed the "Canticle of the Creatures," a hymn of praise and gratitude for the beauty and gifts of creation.  He envisioned all of creation as united in a web of affection and mutual interdependence.  Sister Water, for example, he envisioned as "useful and humble and precious and pure."  Gazing and considering our strained and wounded planet, Pope Francis appealed to Francis's vision of creation at the outset of his encyclical, *Laudato Si': On Care for Our Common Home*, calling us to an integral ecology that will help us ensure a positive future, for ourselves and for our offspring.

                                        *Gillian T.W. Ahlgren*

Embracing St. Francis as "the example par excellence of care for the vulnerable and of an integral ecology lived out joyfully and authentically," Pope Francis helps us to appreciate Francis:

> He was particularly concerned for God's creation and for the poor and outcast. He loved, and was deeply loved for his joy, his generous self-giving, his openheartedness. He was a mystic and a pilgrim who lived in simplicity and in wonderful harmony with God, with others, with nature and with himself. He shows us just how inseparable the bond is between concern for nature, justice for the poor, commitment to society, and interior peace. Francis helps us to see that an integral ecology... takes us to the heart of what it is to be human. (Pope Francis, *On Care for Our Common Home*, pars. 10-11.)

Francis of Assisi shows us that "rather than a problem to be solved, the world is a joyful mystery to be contemplated with gladness and praise." (Pope Francis, *On Care for Our Common Home*, par. 12.) Delighting in the world around us helps us resist cultural pressures to reduce people or nature into things to be consumed, used or controlled. Francis's refusal to objectify the other and his desire to live in solidarity and generosity are two basic human qualities that all of us can choose to develop and express. In fact, solidarity and generosity become increasingly more natural to us as we move through the first three steps of the cycle, because this third step, contemplation, gives us clarity about what we are to do. In the Franciscan paradigm, contemplation leads organically to a fourth step—the solidarity and kinship that result in transformative action in our world.

## STEP 4:
### Discernment and Creative Fidelity

We engage discernment and creative action: Empowered by the

intermediate steps in this process, we move into our lives with clarity about the habits, patterns, and assumptions that need to be rejected in support of human dignity, and we begin the process of change. We seek the deepening of God's life in creation and develop activities that reinforce God's caring presence in our world, strengthening communities for the work ahead. I call this action "fidelity," because it is a critical and integral way of expressing our faithfulness—our fidelity to God, our fidelity to one another, and even to our deepest selves. This way of life helps us to become "capable of seeing the sacred grandeur of our neighbor, of finding God in every human being, of tolerating the nuisances of life in common by clinging to the love of God," opening our hearts to divine love and wisdom, and seeking the happiness of others." (See Pope Francis, *Joy of the Gospel*, par. 92)

While we can certainly call this fourth step "action" (which is how we looked at the word "imitation" in Clare's four verbs above), we need to clarify that this fourth step is "wise action" because it includes what Pope Francis called evangelical discernment—a gospel-informed way of seeing our world and knowing our place in it. Building one another up in a love that inspires growth and demands justice, we witness, in a radiant, practical, and attractive way, what it means to be friend, sister and brother to one another and causing admiration in how we care for, encourage, and accompany each other.

Imitation, the fourth step in our process, is, at root, a reclaiming of our identity as stewards and custodians—caretakers of one another and of our world. Our role as human beings is to appreciate and care for what we have been given—our planet, first and foremost, as well as the lives of all who inhabit it and the treasure of wisdom, insight and creativity handed down to us from age to age. The more that we experience and feel our gratitude for life and our deep belonging to one another, the more we commit to one another's well-being and tap into the creativity and vitality that is

                                   *Gillian T.W. Ahlgren*

God's spirit alive in our world. This spirit gives us the courage to enter spaces where humanity is most wounded, accompanied by the God who is unafraid of the fringes of human existence.

As we have seen through the lives of Francis and Clare, love is the source of that vitality. Love motivates us to move beyond the self. Love gives us the courage to move forward, to gaze upon and consider the injustices in our world. Love helps us find the moral strength to make changes. But many of us have lost confidence in love. The unloving ways of our world have convinced us that love is a fiction, a utopian promise held over us by those who want something from us in the transactional cultures in which we live. Surely that is some of the most dispiriting "false news" on our planet. But love is not dead; it is a living energy, inviting us to open our hearts, engage our world, and create a better way.

Let us allow the shining example of Francis and Clare to guide us forward, not just make us nostalgic for times past. Their vision is a source of wisdom, strength, and life, and it can stimulate us to build up the human community along the lines that they did. Francis and Clare provide a living example of how belonging, commitment, collaboration, creation and thriving are interconnected forms of living out both our relationship to God and our relationship to one another. They show us how to fulfill the one thing that God asks of us: "to act justly, to love tenderly, and to walk humbly with our God." They remind us of the basic observation: "No one can serve two masters. Either you will hate the one and love the other or you will be devoted to the one and despise the other." (See Matthew 6:24 and Luke 16:13-15.) We today experience this tension at least as strongly as Francis and Clare did. They recognized the cultural pressures that kept them from experiencing the God who wanted to come alive, in them and in the world around them. They chose instead to take a long, loving look at the world around them and respond, in love, to the God who invited them to try another way.

Will we today respond to their invitation to us to gaze and consider the suffering in our world, to contemplate it with God, to trace the suffering in the world down to the roots of injustice, plucking them out and enacting the call of the gospel to solidarity and mutual accountability?  Are we clear enough yet that the ways that we more typically live are neither life-giving nor fulfilling?  Is that enough to motivate us to make the changes that we and our world need?

The metanoia inspired by Francis and Clare will require us to move beyond superficial rhetoric, sporadic acts of philanthropy and perfunctory expressions of concern for the environment in a paradigmatic shift with deep, transformative implications for us and for our world.  As Pope Francis observed, the universal communion modeled by Francis and Clare

> should make us particularly indignant at the enormous inequalities in our midst, whereby we continue to tolerate some people considering themselves more worthy than others. We fail to see that some are mired in desperate and degrading poverty, with no way out, while others have not the faintest idea of what to do with their possessions, vainly showing off their supposed superiority... In practice, we continue to tolerate that some consider themselves more human than others, as if they had been born with greater rights. (Pope Francis, *On Care for Our Common Home*, par. 90.)

Such a metanoia will require a re-evaluation of the sense of entitlement that so many people today feel, as the language of "rights" becomes completely detached from the language of "responsibilities."  Spurred on by a loving awareness that we are not disconnected from the rest of creation, we can find both the courage to care and the courage to change in the ways that the common good requires of us.  If we allow our desire to live with generosity of spirit to be strengthened by the sense of urgency that we feel about things in our world that aren't working, we may yet be able to find the collective will to work toward the common good.

Francis and Clare help us to see that the "conversion" we are speaking of is not a movement toward greater religiosity, but toward deepening integrity and relational commitment, to God and to one another. Francis and Clare also show us that the changes that God invites us to make are forms of freedom— freedom from and freedom for. Freedom from all that diminishes our human dignity, individually and collectively; freedom for a life of integrity, committed to a way of relatedness that brings life, even when we are deprived of all else. Both their radical poverty and their tenderness, which gave them access to the full range of their humanity, set a standard for us as a people who choose to stand together in the constant and secretly interwoven relationships that bind us to one another.

As we uncover our intrinsic relatedness, we "not only marvel at the manifold connections existing among creatures, but also discover a key to our own fulfillment. The human person grows more, matures more and is sanctified more to the extent that he or she enters into relationships, going out from themselves to live in communion with God, with others and with all creatures." (Pope Francis, *On Care for Our Common Home*, par. 240.)

There are many serious issues that need to be addressed and remediated. A new and universal solidarity would need to express itself in the cooperative construction of new systems of interaction, new ways of living together, along with legal frameworks that can guarantee human rights and a global ethos that demands and requires mutual accountabilities. From human trafficking to gender-based violence and abuse to racism, exploitation, exclusion, and care for our fragile planet, we may easily find ourselves wondering where and how to begin. The injustices in our world easily spawn "a lethal absence of hope," and our task is to use God's own loving gaze at the spaces of horror and degradation to create new communities of vitality and life. Pope Francis put this poignantly over a decade ago:

> How I wish that all of us would hear God's cry: "Where is your brother?" (Gn 4:9). Where is your brother or sister who is enslaved? Where is the brother and sister that you are killing each day in clandestine warehouses, in rings of prostitution, in children used for begging, in exploiting undocumented labor. Let us not look the other way. There is greater complicity than we think. (Pope Francis, *Joy of the Gospel*, par. 211.)

The rewards for the changes we make may not be initially obvious to us, because the walls of exclusion in our societies are strong enough to keep us from understanding or experiencing the richness on the other side of them. Encounter is what enriches our lives, and we will not discover it if we do not go beyond ourselves. If we recall Francis's initial experience in the leper colony, we remember that this was the space in which he himself was flooded with the love of God. What he expected to be a space of misery and abandonment was, to his surprise, a space of vitality, where human relatedness, care and compassion had the capacity to change everything.

As Greg Boyle reminds us, the space of encounter at the margins is a space of privilege. Our voluntary displacement with the oppressed, with those whose burdens make it nearly impossible for them to even cry out for the help they need, gives us a life-changing perspective that we cannot find on our own:



*Gillian T. W. Ahlgren*

The poor give you a privileged access to the God who stands there with them. Once you experience this, it is where you want to reside... If you listen to the poor and those on the margins, they will tell you what needs to be done. (Greg Boyle, *Tattoos on the Heart*, pp. 229, 225)

We can begin simply, with individual and communal practices of gazing, considering, and contemplating in all areas of daily life. These practices support larger shifts from life-threatening habits to a sharing of the love that gives life. The process is basic but it also becomes the basis for the revolution in thinking, acting and loving that we and our world need. Broadly applicable and consistent with other practical methods for integrating theological insights, spirituality and ethical action, the four concrete steps in this method enable us to journey together in the way of Francis and Clare, creating lives of meaning and purpose in which we recognize and honor the possibilities embedded in our common humanity. These steps can be used by individuals, groups, communities, both as a way to embrace life more purposefully and as a way to understand the world around us and fruitfully transform it according to the promptings of God's living Spirit.

*   *   *

We live in the context of challenges that require us to change. We can throw up our hands at the chaos and dysfunction of our world or we can challenge ourselves to reclaim together all that is being lost through our insensitivities, indifference and intransigence.

Yet all is not lost. Human beings, while capable of the worst, are also capable of rising above themselves, choosing again what is good, and making a new start, despite their mental and social conditioning. We are able to take an honest look at ourselves, to acknowledge our deep dissatisfaction, and to embark on new paths to authentic freedom. No system can completely suppress our openness to what is good, true and beautiful, or our God-given ability to respond to the grace at work deep in our hearts. I appeal to everyone throughout the world not to forget this dignity which is ours. No one has the right to take it from us. (Pope Francis, *On Care for Our Common Home*, par. 205.)

As Francis and Clare showed us, God's tenderness is meant to manifest itself in all of our forms of human relatedness as an integral part of our journey as human beings. Its hallmarks are justice, dignity, mutual respect, and powerful cherishing. This tenderness makes us approach others with immense respect, a desire for their deepest freedom and fruition, and a hopeful anticipation of what is possible when we embody our deepest human values. The times in which we live require this tenderness with a new and powerful urgency, since it will help us navigate the profound changes that lie ahead.

The legacy of Francis and Clare is their invitation into an authentic, all-encompassing, gospel-informed way of life. This legacy is grounded in a God-centered vision of humanity and the world that manifests and engenders tenderness, reverence, justice, simplicity, peace, and joy. Francis's and Clare's relational way of life shows us how to be together in human community. They reinforce the basic human need for embracing a simplicity of life that allows us to develop the richness of our relatedness. This richness exposes the truth that we experience today: We are not made happier by too many choices, too much stuff, and the tyranny of the urgent ruling our lives. Francis and Clare's radical simplicity enabled them to live in gratitude, joy and even abundance of divine presence.

The paradox and mystery of Francis's and Clare's poverty is that it completely redefines their experience of humanity. To live in



*Gillian T.W. Ahlgren*

poverty is to live in acute awareness of our need for God, our desire for God—and for one another. Francis's and Clare's poverty is the poverty of incompletion that invites us into relational fullness, that draws us into a new identity, one defined by solidarity, mutuality and the dynamic fruition of holiness as we explore, together, the presence of God in our midst. As we let go of our need to possess both things and people, we are freed to feel the presence of God and to orient our lives toward that presence, dwelling in it and sharing it as our deepest, truest reality.

This freedom also allows us to learn the power of love and its capacity to encourage and uphold us through time and space. Francis and Clare had little conversation or even contact, and yet they were able to cultivate and nurture a profound and prayerful, supportive relationship. In the quiet spaces of their own hearts, they knew that they could always find the loving prayers of the other to uphold them in their integrity and heart-felt sincerity to live out their relationship with God. They were custodians of one another's souls, and the union with God that each of them enjoyed was a shared union, a communion with one another. If that tender, "providential" care and regard for the other were at the heart of every committed human relationship today, our world would be a very different place. For the love that burned in each of their hearts was magnified by the knowledge that there was another human being on this earth who knew, understood, and revered that fire as sacred. Knowing love with this kind of intensity and even purity pulls love out of the realm of sentimentality and restores it rightfully to its place of ultimate power. It is the kind of love that dispels the idolatrous ways that we perceive and enact power in our world.

As Pope Francis reminded us over a decade ago, loving others is "a spiritual force drawing us to union with God," and love is, in the end, the only light that "can always illuminate a world grown dim and give us the courage needed to keep living and working…. We do not live better when we flee, hide, refuse to share, stop giving and lock ourselves up in our own comforts. Such a life is nothing less than a slow suicide." (See Pope Francis, Joy of the Gospel, par. 272) Francis and Clare show us that meaning, purpose and joy can only be found when hopes, dreams, challenges, and all that makes us human is shared. The vitality they gained as they shared God's dream for all creation can give us today the courage we need if we are going to meet our culture with realism and fill it with life-giving love.

Francis and Clare invite us into a way of life in which loving others is a desire that unites us to God and stems naturally from the knowledge that we are loved. It is a way of loving grown in us as we come to understand that we are all sisters and brothers, children of the same Source. Greg Boyle describes this core relationality very simply, calling it "kinship," which he defines as what happens to us when we refuse to forget that we belong to each other. "With kinship as the goal," he writes, "other essential things fall into place; without it, no justice, no peace. I suspect that were kinship our goal, we would no longer be promoting justice—we would be celebrating it." (Greg Boyle, *Tattoos on the Heart*, p. 187) Kinship is not service, and it is not charity. Kinship, like solidarity, is mutuality, known as we share vulnerability, joy, challenge, hopes, dreams, and desires. It is the shared space where the tenderness that formed us calls us home.



*Gillian T.W. Ahlgren*

# Bibliography

## Primary Sources on Francis and Clare

Francis of Assisi. *Early Documents*, 3 vols., ed. Regis J. Armstrong, New York: New City Press, 1999-2004.

*Clare of Assisi: The Lady. Early Documents*, ed. Regis J. Armstrong. New York: New City Press, 2006.

Clare of Assisi. *The Letters to Agnes*, trans. Joan Mueller. Michael Glazier, 2003.

Bonaventure. *The Soul's Journey into God, The Tree of Life, The Life of St. Francis*, trans. Ewert Cousins. New York: Paulist Press, 1978.

## Secondary Sources on Francis and Clare

Maria Pia Alberzoni. *Clare of Assisi and the Poor Sisters in the Thirteenth Century*. St. Bonaventure, NY: Franciscan Institute Publications, 2004.

Murray Bodo. *The Way of St. Francis: The Challenge of Franciscan Spirituality for Everyone*. New York: Image Books, 1995.

Leonardo Boff. *Francis of Assisi: A Model for Human Liberation*. Trans. John W. Diercksmeier. Maryknoll, NY: Orbis Books, 2006.

Jacques Dalarun. *Francis of Assisi and Power*. Saint Bonaventure, NY: Franciscan Institute Publications, 2007.

______. *Francis of Assisi and the Feminine*. Saint Bonaventure, NY: Franciscan Institute Publications, 2006.

______. *The Misadventure of Francis of Assisi: Toward a Historical*

*Use of the Franciscan Legends*. St. Bonaventure, NY: Franciscan Institute Publications, 2002.

Ilia Delio, *Clare of Assisi: A Heart Full of Love*. Cincinnati, OH: St. Anthony Messenger Press, 2007.

______. *Franciscan Prayer*. Cincinnati: St. Anthony Messenger Press, 2004.

______. *A Franciscan View of Creation: Learning to Live in a Sacramental World*. St. Bonaventure, NY: The Franciscan Institute, 2003.

______, Keith Douglass Warner, and Pamela Wood. *Care for Creation: A Franciscan Spirituality of the Earth*. Cincinnati: St. Anthony Messenger Press, 2008

Chiara Frugoni. *Francis of Assisi: A Life*. New York: Continuum, 1998.

M. D. Lambert. *Franciscan Poverty: The Doctrine of the Absolute Poverty of Christ and the Apostles in the Franciscan Order (1210-1323)*. St. Bonaventure, NY: Franciscan Institute Publications, 1998.

Raoul Manselli. *Saint Francis of Assisi*. Chicago, 1988.

Joan Mueller. *The Privilege of Poverty: Clare of Assisi, Agnes of Prague, and the Struggle for a Franciscan Rule for Women*. Philadelphia: The Pennsylvania State University Press, 2007.


**Pilgrimage Resources**

Theophile Desbonnets. *Assisi in the Footsteps of St. Francis: A Spiritual Guidebook*, trans. Nancy Celaschi. Assisi: Edizioni Porziuncola, 1993.

Roch Niemier, *In the Footsteps of Francis and Clare*. Cincinnati: St. Antony Messenger Press, 2006.

　　　　　　　　　　　　　　*Gillian T. W. Ahlgren*

# About the Author

Gillian T. W. Ahlgren is Professor Emerita of Theology at Xavier University, where she began teaching in 1990. She received her Ph.D. from the University of Chicago in the History of Christianity with a specialization in the Christian mystical tradition. In addition to teaching graduate and undergraduate courses in theology, the history of Christianity, and Christian spirituality, she designs and facilitates retreats and immersive experiences that support personal and social transformation.

A widely published author, her previous books include *Teresa of Avila and the Politics of Sanctity* (Cornell University Press, 1996), *Entering Teresa of Avila's Interior Castle: A Reader's Companion* (Paulist Press, 2005), *The Inquisition of Francisca: A Sixteenth-Century Visionary on Trial* (University of Chicago Press, 2005), *Enkindling Love: The Legacy of Teresa of Avila and John of the Cross* (Fortress Press, 2016), *The Tenderness of God: Reclaiming Our Humanity* (Fortress Press, 2017), *Spiritual Exercises for the 21st Century: A Workbook* (third edition VITALITY, 2025), *Palace Within: Exploring Teresa of Avila's Interior Castle* (VITALITY, 2025), and *Faces of Metanoia* (VITALITY, 2026). Dr. Ahlgren is internationally known for her work on the Christian mystical tradition and regularly gives public lectures, retreats and workshops on various figures in Christian spirituality and their wisdom for living today.

In addition to her work as a scholar and teacher, Dr. Ahlgren has been engaged in pastoral work at a variety of levels. After training in spiritual direction at the Center for Religious Development in 2005, she began to design and facilitate retreats, especially with those at the margins. In 2009 she was a founding member of the

Cincinnati Women's Team of the Ignatian Spirituality Project, a national organization providing spiritual accompaniment for formerly homeless women in recovery from substance abuse. Since 2013 she has incorporated wisdom from Teresa's Interior Castle and other classic spiritual texts in her work with women who have survived domestic violence.

Dr. Ahlgren is available to facilitate workshops, training programs, immersions, and retreats. She periodically offers week-long Spiritual Immersion Experiences in the Footsteps of Francis and Clare in Assisi, in the Footsteps of Teresa in Avila, and in the Spiritual Exercises.

Please visit her website at **www.gillianahlgren.com** or contact her at **ahlgren@xavier.edu**.

Contemplative Wisdom for Today is a series dedicated to making the wisdom of the Christian mystical tradition accessible as a source of practical wisdom for life today. Using the lives and teachings of visionary leaders in Christian spirituality, we support spiritual growth through reading circles, workshops, and even offer spiritual immersion experiences in Assisi, Avila, Norwich and Santiago de Compostela.

For more information, please visit
**www.contemplativewisdomfortoday.org.**

# VITALITY

growing love,
sharing holistic self-care,
and inspiring creative expression.

We invite you to explore with us through our
affordable, friendly drop-in classes…
in person & online

**vitalitycincinnati.org**

and our books

**vitalitybuzz.org**